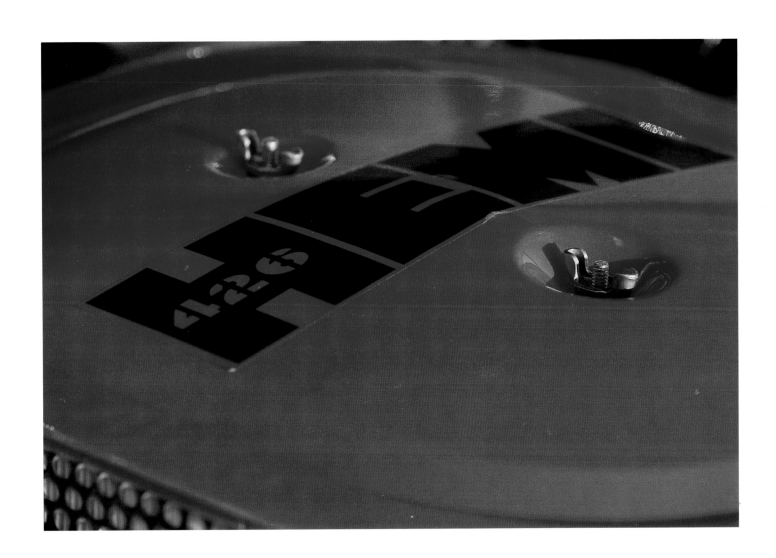

MOPAR MUSCLE

FIFTY YEARS

DODGE, PLYMOUTH & CHRYSLER PERFORMANCE

ROBERT GENAT
PHOTOGRAPHY BY DAVID NEWHARDT

MOTORBOOKS
INTERNATIONAL

To Randy Leffingwell:

An excellent automotive journalist and a wonderful friend to both of us.

First published in 2004 by Motorbooks International, an imprint of MBI Publishing Company, Galtier Plaza, Suite 200, 380 Jackson Street, St. Paul, MN 55101-3885 USA

ISBN 0-7603-2016-0

Edited by: Darwin Holmstrom
Layout by: Brenda Canales

Endpaper: The Hemi engine was perhaps the finest tire shredding device ever invented.

On the cover: The "T/A" in the name of Dodge's Challenger T/A stood for "Trans Am," the race series in which the car was designed to compete.

On the frontispiece: The Hemi engine needed a lot of air flowing through its combustion chambers to light up the huge quantities of gas gulped by its dual four-barrel carburetors.

On the title page: Sublime was one of the many vivid colors that could be selected for a 1970 Road Runner.

On the back cover: (main) The 1966 Plymouth Belvedere's styling featured squared-off lines that were dated compared to its Ford and GM contemporaries. Goodyear Blue Streak tires are the first indication this Plymouth is powered by a Hemi. *(indication)* By 1969 Dodge had shed its stodgy styling. It's Coke bottle-shaped B-body cars were some of the sleekest vehicles on the road. *(indication)* Dodge reached into its past when designing the graphics for the Hemi-powered Rumble Bee pickup. *(indication)* Shod with huge 18-inch BBS wheels, the 1998 GTS-R was a street-legal race car, packing 460 horsepower. Sometimes called a GT2, it was the road-going clone of the factory GTS-R race car. Slotted vents on the hood were functional.

Printed in China

MOPAR MUSCLE FIFTY YEARS

5

ACKNOWLEDGMENTS

My deepest appreciation and heartfelt thanks go out to my friend and co-author Dave Newhardt. We met several years ago at a book signing I was doing in San Diego. Since then, we've become the best of friends. We were both born and raised in the Midwest, we both spent time in the Navy (he was in the real Navy, I was in the floor-buffer Navy), we both have supportive wives, and we both live life with the same set of values. In 30 years of taking photographs, I've learned more about photography from him than anyone else. He brings his classically trained eye to the automotive world. It's a fresh and innovative look that begs for "the big screen" freedom offered by a book like this one. His photos are not just of the vehicles, but of the sexy curves they possess and of the emotion they generate. He artfully integrates the car with its surroundings. Throughout this project I have been calling him "Master and Commander." He's the master of taking a poor location and transforming it into an artful setting. He is the commander of light and his photography is pure art. Dave is the most inventive photographer I've ever met. Throughout the course of this project he would call me with outlandish ideas for new camera mounts and with ideas for adding motion to his photos. I'm always amazed by how his photographs draw the viewer in. I'm deeply honored and proud to share this book with him. No one could have captured these beautiful cars better than my dear friend David Newhardt. Great job, Dave.

I must also thank Tom Gale for writing the eloquent to foreword to this book. When I went to Tom's home in Michigan to interview him, I expected to be there for only two or three hours at most. Twelve hours later, after a lovely afternoon and dinner, I was on my way. In addition to being a former vice president of Chrysler, he is a grease-under-the-fingernails gearhead. He owns a hot rod, a muscle car, and a Viper, and he can speak with authority on the history, styling, and mechanics of each type of vehicle. I'm proud to have his voice as part of this book. Thanks, again, Tom.

Thanks to the following cars owners who gave freely of their time and cars: Kenn Funk, Kahlena Funk, David Hakim, Joe Trotta, Earl Brown, Tom Gale, Harold Sullivan, Steve and Nancy Atwell, John Lazenby, John Hadgis, and Mark Farrin. Their dedication to the preservation of these wonderful cars gives this book special historical value.

With any project of this size, there are always people who support me in a variety of ways to pull the project together. They do this by giving me research materials, referrals, a sanity check, or a roof over my head; consenting to an interview; or serving as a model or an advisor. Thanks to: Gordie and Connie Craig, Jessica Sepulveda, Richard Petty, Gary Jankowski, Wally Parks, John Hertog, Gil Cunningham, Mike Porto, Bill Maloney, Jim Burr, and Larry Weiner.

Without the cooperation of the wonderful people at DaimlerChrysler, this book could not have happened. Thanks to Dieter Zetsche, Terri Houtman, Joe Trotta, Todd Goyer, Lisa Barrow, David Hakim, Lori Pinter, Dan Knott, Brandt Rosenbusch, Robert Lee, Cole Quinnell, Scott Wilkins, John Opfer, Joe Grace, Burke Brown, Bob Longstreth, Rick Deneau, Heather May, and Bryan Zvibleman.

—Robert Genat
Encinitas, California
2004

Every so often, an automotive photographer is blessed to work on a project covering a wide range of subjects that just stops them in their tracks. This is one of those—filled with a lot of personal "Oh my God" moments, when an automobile, through design, lighting, and setting, becomes sculpture on wheels. None of this would have been possible without the help of the vehicle owners, who put up with my requests with resigned good humor and came away with a sense, after looking in the camera viewfinder, that maybe they really do own something special. You're damn right you do, and I warmly thank all of you!

Kenn Funk, Chuck Smith, Red Kilby, Sean Machado, David Mikkekon, Julius "Restorations By Julius" Steuer, Lou Kanellis, Maria Kanellis, Bill Kanellis, Ron Flacxinski, Ed Dea, Mark Farrin, Erik Baltzar, Joe Van Fleet, John Lazenby, John Wilkiewicz, Aaron Kahlenberg, Donald A. Lewis, Jeff and Kristy Peters, Bill Sams, Ken Katarynchuk, Blake Machine, Craig Jackson, Steve Davis, Jerry Gleich, Rick Melms, Rob Lelakowski, Richard Rowlands, Steve Atwell, John Marconi, Denis Fedler, Michael Schultz, Brandt Rosenbusch, Norm Ver Hage, Ken Soto, Bob Gough, Doug Coull, Jack Berdasko, Harold Sullivan, and David Henriksen.

On the payroll at DaimlerChrysler are a group of automotive enthusiasts—Dan Knott, Todd Goyer, Dan Bodene, Shannon T. Carr, Cole Quinnell, Mary Beth Halprin, and Dean Reifsnider— who love what they do and are great at it. They allowed me access to automobiles that stir the soul and make me very pleased that I work in this business. Without their help, this book would have been *Mopar Muscle Lite*. Thank you for the opportunity to see some of the treasures behind the curtain, both old and new. You folks have a wonderful toy box! Last, but by no means least, is DaimlerChrysler's Western Region PR hotshoe, Lisa Barrow, who smoothes the waters, opens the doors, and tosses us the keys.

Automotive photographers are indebted to a lot of people who toil behind the scenes, allowing us access to locations, modeling, and moral support. Without these people's help, I would have been reduced to shooting in parks and driveways. Thank you Doug Stokes, Irwindale Speedway, Katee Foxx, Shannon N. Schilling, Jessica Sepulveda, the crew at The Nest, Mike Smyth, Dick Messer and Leslie Kendall of the Petersen Automotive Museum, Mark Perleberg, N.A.D.A Appraisal Guides, Bob Tate, and the Walter P. Chrysler Museum.

My co-conspirator in this book, Robert Genat, has been a friend for years, and it was an overdue pleasure working with him. I'm ready for Round II Robert! A big Thank You must be extended to MBI's Darwin Holmstrom, our editor. Had I been in his shoes, it would have gotten ugly. His job is like herding cats, a thankless task. I appreciate all of your help.

Finally, I want to thank my wife, Susan J. Foxx-Newhardt, for her patience as I chased Mopars all over the country. Yes, dear, you'll look great behind the wheel of a Crossfire Roadster.

—David W. Newhardt
Pasadena, California
2004

FOREWORD

The ever-changing landscape at Chrysler Corporation had a profound effect on the development and spirit of its products. Throughout the years management structures, economic cycles, and perhaps most importantly the spirit of handfuls of loyalists to various causes within the organization influenced this landscape. This book vividly illustrates how much things can change in the product world of automobiles when inspired people create products that either lead or react to the environment within which they operate.

My tenure at Chrysler spanned a significant portion of the era that is addressed in the following pages, and I was a first-hand observer of the corporation's performance products during my youth, both on the streets and at the drag strips. It would be difficult to miss that something dramatic was happening at Chrysler in the early 1950s, with the Italian-bodied Virgil Exner–era show cars, the C300 in 1955, and some of the most dramatic designs in the industry in 1957. The high-performance image, the designs, and the legendary Hemi engines all contributed to the spawning of a culture in the product organization that was very evident when I joined the company in advance engineering in 1967.

Those early years of Chrysler performance brought us drag strip results so astounding that it literally forced competitive reaction. And time and time again the small band of zealots would bring product to get the job done and command the respect of competitors. The early 1960s "wedge" engines in relatively light B bodies and the small-block A-bodied Dart and Valiant cars began to set the stage for what was to come.

In the mid-1960s, it was the High Banks–inspired race Hemi engines and the street engines that followed—which ranged from Hemis to multi-carbed small-block engines—that provided all the materials needed for a talented group of planners and designers to create amazing results that are coveted to this day.

A significant and ground-breaking aerodynamics group conspired with designers to bring the Charger 500, the Daytona, and of course the "winged cars" by the end of the decade. During this time the parking lot at the end of the styling building would always contain some of the most interesting vehicles on the planet. These were the cars that belonged to the studio chiefs and other product executives. I can remember the Charger 500 of Carl Cameron with his special outline bumble bee graphic and of course, John Herlitz's Hemi 'Cuda convertible in triple black, just to name two.

In the late 1960s we were working on the cars that ultimately were some of the best ever created. The 1968 B-body Charger R/T, Cornet R/T, Super Bee, GTX, and Roadrunner were outstanding in terms of design, performance, and ultimately the image they brought to the company. The sales results were also enough to give credence to this new era of performance, and led to the development of a new range of pony cars that would have the ultimate range of capability. This new series of vehicles coded internally as the F-series E-body models would have all-new sheet metal and the entire range of engines from the biggest of big blocks to the slant six.

These 1970 Barracuda/Challenger models were the first vehicles I worked on as a young engineer, and the experience was unbelievable for a car nut who grew up in General Motors' heartland of Flint, Michigan. I can vividly remember seeing the first prototype of one of the Trans Am–inspired AAR 'Cudas and Challenger T/As in the engineering paint shop and thinking to myself that someday I would have to have one of my very own. (There was definitely something in the water of Highland Park that caused so many of us to labor toward those lofty goals that only car guys or gals would understand.)

Indeed, the spirit in Highland Park made the troops proud, but the forces of regulation in the form of emissions and fuel economy would also have a significant voice in the environmental equation. There were just not enough years to recapture the significant capital investments of the new

models aimed at the performance market before insurance and mandated regulatory issues dampened consumer enthusiasm. The era of the 1970s and even the early 1980s are sometimes called "the forgotten years," and perhaps that is the kindest term we can give because they were extremely tough times at Chrysler Corporation.

The oil shocks of 1974 and 1979 changed the environment for products and ultimately the technologies, but never diminished the desire for outstanding and remarkable performance products. In 1978 and 1979 we had new leaders named Hal Sperlich and Lee Iacocca who would form a new band of executives that would ultimately pave the way for an exciting resurgence of the proud Chrysler Corporation. This resurgence would start in the mid-1980s and continue through the 1990s, bringing us some of the most exciting products in the company's history.

The K-cars and minivans provided the fuel to acquire American Motors and Jeep brands in 1987. The management organization formed the first product teams responsible for reinventing not only the products, but also the method in which we worked. This proved extremely successful by any measure, but most importantly, it rekindled the performance spirit and ultimately led to products like the Viper, Prowler, PT Cruiser, and all of the ground-breaking next-generation minivans, Jeeps, cab-forward sedans, and Ram trucks. People in the organization believed in their instincts and intuitive feel for how much was enough and how much was too much.

Today we have come full circle to the new Chrysler 300C and Dodge Magnum, very much inspired by the originals, and of course the Hemi that evokes so many images of the past. This circling back to the rich performance heritage of a company that provided so many enthusiasts with very gratifying careers raises very strong emotions, especially among the insiders. Hopefully, this book will illustrate and explain those strong feelings, as expressed through the products and the people of an amazing 50 years.

—Tom Gale

Tom Gale is one of those brilliant auto executives who had a crystal clear vision of the future, and an unambiguous understanding of the past. His personal muscle car is this Lemon Twist AAR 'Cuda.

9

INTRODUCTION

In the early 1960s, I frequently went to Detroit Dragway to watch the Super Stock cars drag race. The track announcer always referred to Plymouths and Dodges as "Mopars." I heard that word so many times that I thought there must be a division of Chrysler that produced Plymouth and Dodge race cars branded as Mopar. Eventually, I became aware of the fact that Chrysler's parts division was named Mopar.

The Mopar name came about in 1937. Nelson Farley was the head of Chrysler's brand sales promotion. He asked his employees to come up with a catchy name for a new line of antifreeze products. The one he chose was a combination of the words MOtor PARts—MOPAR. The name stuck and eventually became a catchall phrase for any Chrysler product, whether vehicle or parts.

The name Mopar would not have had any distinction had it not been attached to a good product. Over the years, Chrysler produced some of the most outstanding high-performance cars ever built. In 1951 Chrysler introduced its first 331-ci Hemi engine rated at 180 horsepower. By 1955 the Hemi's horsepower rating had ballooned to 300. Chrysler built its C300 around that engine and the legend began.

Throughout the years, each successive Chrysler car grew in horsepower, further cementing the association of the word "Mopar" with high performance. The timing was perfect. In the early 1960s, drag racing and NASCAR held the attention of America's auto racing fans. The new generation of Mopar wedge engines swept over the drag strips like a tornado through a Kansas trailer park. Unfortunately, they were not up to the task of winning the longer 500-mile NASCAR races. It would take the introduction of a new Hemi engine to accomplish that task. In February 1964, Richard Petty won the Daytona 500 in his 426-Hemi-powered Plymouth hardtop. Racing would never be the same.

Hemi-powered Mopars dominated NASCAR racing and the drag strips. In order to conform to the rules of NASCAR competition, the Hemi engine had to be something that anyone could purchase at a local dealership. The street Hemi was born, creating another chapter in Mopar performance history. Between 1966 and 1971, these powerful engines were sold in such classic cars as the Road Runner and Hemi 'Cuda—both icons of the muscle car era. Also dominating the muscle car world in the late 1960s and early 1970s were the Super Bee, Dodge Charger R/T, Coronet R/T, Challenger R/T, and Plymouth GTX. But in 1970, looming emission standards and high insurance surcharges were growing like a fungus in a Petri dish.

By the end of the 1971 model year, the double-knotted noose of insurance surcharges and emission laws had tightened, choking the breath out of the muscle car era. Soon gasoline would be in short supply, and while people still wanted big-block high performance cars, the costs associated with owning such beasts became prohibitive. Chrysler had the foresight—or luck—to produce a wonderful selection of A-bodied Swingers, Dusters, and Demons. Powered by the stout 340-ci Mopar small block, these cars offered a great deal of performance at a bargain price.

In the 1970s Chrysler almost bled to death as its inventory of large, gas-guzzling cars failed to move off dealership lots. The mushroom cloud of fuel shortages, along with a shaky economy, left cars on lots for months. By 1980, automotive analysts predicted Chrysler's steep downward spiral would soon terminate in a smoking crater. But then in rode Lee Iacocca—a white knight with a big stogie in his mouth and a strong desire to make Chrysler succeed.

Lee Iacocca had been booted out of his mahogany-lined Ford Motor Company office and joined Chrysler to save the company and get a little revenge. To save the company he met Congress face-to-face and asked for a loan to keep the company afloat. Even though he shunned the limelight, he took center stage in television ads placing his—and the company's—reputation on the line. The front-wheel-drive K-cars and mini vans that saved the company may not have been glamorous, but they were functional and seemed to be what the public wanted—and also saved thousands of jobs. The

Harold Sullivan owns one of the finest collections of Mopar muscle cars in the nation. Here in his Detroit-area shop, he details a Hemi engine that will soon be installed in his 1971 Challenger R/T convertible.

success of the new K-cars allowed Iacocca to pay back the government loan long before it was due.

As the 1990s began there was a feeling of hope within Chrysler. Designers and engineers had proven that they could produce a good car. Now they wanted to produce an exciting car. First built as a concept vehicle, the Viper became the hottest and most powerful American sports car ever built. The Viper took on legendary status, as had the Hemi engine before it.

The creation of the Viper was a great confidence builder for Chrysler. Encouraged, the company took on the hot rod world by building the first production car that looked like a street rod. The Prowler, a low-slung, two-seat, open-wheeled roadster, was unlike any car ever built in an American factory. This gave Chrysler the confidence to create another retro-styled vehicle—the PT Cruiser. It, too, was a success.

But behind the scenes at the 1998 North American Auto Show a discussion took place that would change automotive history. Jurgen E. Schrempp, chairman of the Daimler-Benz Management Board, approached Bob Eaton, chairman and chief executive officer of Chrysler, and suggested a possible merger. A month later a small group of representatives from both companies started discussions. Through March and April 1998, teams from both companies hammered out the details. On May 6, 1998 the merger agreement was signed and the next day announced to the public. On September 18, 1998, shareholders from both companies voted by a wide majority to approve the merger. On November 17, 1998, DaimlerChrysler stock began to trade world wide under the symbol DCX.

As the year 2000 dawned, DaimlerChrysler was back in the high-performance car world. Technology sharing would benefit cars built on both sides of the Atlantic Ocean. Within a few years, a new Hemi engine was manufactured, four-cylinder Neons were running the quarter mile at speeds of over 100 miles per hour, and a pickup truck was powered with a Viper engine. The free sharing of technology and proven components led to the Crossfire, Chrysler's first two-seat sports car. The new Hemi-powered 300C and Dodge Magnum also benefited from Mercedes' deep parts bins.

Performance has always been in the DNA of Chrysler employees. Because of changing laws, fuel shortages and economic conditions, innovators had to wait for the right time for new projects. In the 1950s performance took the form of the 300 letter cars; in the 1960s and 1970s it took the form of the Road Runner, Super Bee, Charger, 'Cuda, and Challenger.

Today, DaimlerChrysler's performance, spirit, and innovation are showcased in the impressive SRT-badged vehicles that span the automotive landscape from the compact-tuner Neon to the Viper-powered pickup to the new Hemi 300C. Down the road, Chrysler will no doubt develop more breathtaking vehicles that redefine the notion of automotive performance. And enthusiasts will always call them Mopars!

Chrysler's SRT (Street and Racing Technology) organization is responsible for developing its motorsports engineering programs. Its current fleet of performance vehicles includes the Neon SRT-4, Ram SRT-10, Viper SRT-10, and Crossfire SRT-6.

The 1955 Chrysler C-300's standard interior featured chair-height seats covered in soft tan leather.

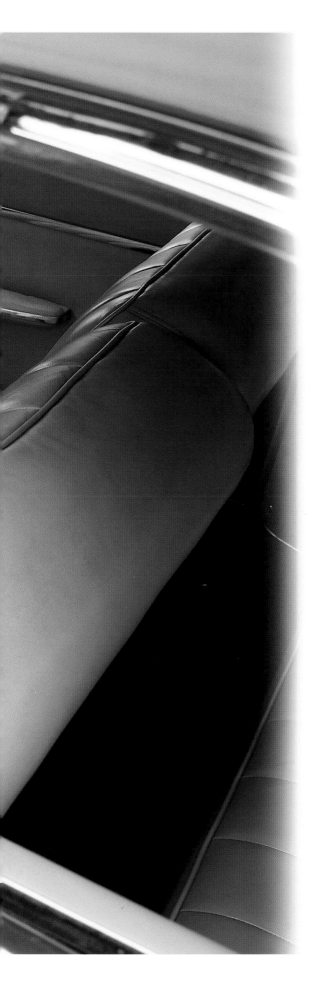

Chrysler 300:

AMERICA'S FIRST PERFORMANCE SEDAN

Chrysler's Hemi development coincided with a renaissance in automotive styling. Since the demise of the Airflow in 1937, Chrysler had been apprehensive about taking any chances with exterior design. In the postwar years, Chrysler's design philosophy consisted of placing a smaller box on top of a larger box. These big square machines, with their flat windshields and exterior door handles that opened with a twist, were practical to a fault. While Chrysler had an outstanding engine, the styling of its cars needed a shot of steroids. That shot came from designer Virgil Exner.

In 1949, Tex Colbert brought Exner in to head the company's Advanced Studio. Exner wrestled the development of new car styling away from the engineers and placed it in the hands of designers. Soon after, auto shows featured Chrysler "Idea Cars": exotic machines such as the Chrysler d'Elegance, the DeSoto Adventurer, and the Dodge Firearrow. Designed in Detroit, these cars of the future were built by Italian coachbuilder Ghia. Exner favored the beauty of European designs, which he felt evolved from the elegant coaches used by European royalty. He believed the American cars evolved from the rugged stagecoach—a sturdy, oversize box in which the common man could pack all his belongings and travel long distances. All Chrysler's products of the 1950s benefited from Exner's soft design touch.

In 1955, the American automotive industry broke all records by selling 9,204,049 units. In addition to record sales numbers, 1955 proved a monumental year in the history and development of

The 1955 Chrysler C-300 proved that an elegant and understated design could succeed in an era of flamboyant cars and color schemes. The C-300 sat one-inch lower than the other 1955 Chryslers due to its heavy-duty suspension. Chrome wire wheels were an option.

The front of the 1956 Chrysler 300-B featured the same bold grille as the 1955 model except for the addition of the letter "B" to the front emblem.

the American automobile. Chevrolet saved the fledgling Corvette from extinction by gracing the two-seat sports car with its newly introduced 265 ci V-8 engine. Ford entered the sports car scrum with its V-8 powered Thunderbird. Chrysler didn't have the money to build a sports car. Instead it converted a Chrysler sedan into a sporty car and the C-300 was born.

The 1955 Chrysler C-300 was 10 years ahead of the curve, presaging such sporty four-passenger coupes as the Buick Riviera, Olds Toronado, and Ford Thunderbird. The timing was right and the excellent package Chrysler put together combined smart styling with a legendary engine. With its 300 horsepower, the C-300 kicked open the door to the muscle car era.

In 1955, Chrysler spent $100 million redesigning its entire line of cars. To facilitate this, Chrysler President Tex Colbert acquired $250 million from Prudential in a 100-year loan. This massive loan was necessary because Chrysler's cars were miserably outdated. The success of the design of Chrysler's entire line of 1955 cars rested on Virgin Exner's shoulders.

1955 C-300

On January 17, 1955 Chrysler announced the C-300, the only Chrysler letter-car that would have the letter prefix (later iterations would have the letter as a suffix). Chrysler's introduction timing coincided with the Daytona Speed and Performance trials. Within a month, new Chrysler C-300s would be rolling off the assembly line.

After a visit to Mexico to watch the LaCarrera Panamericana road race, Chrysler's chief research engineer Bob Rodger conceived building a sporty version of Chrysler's basic sedan. In August 1954, Rodger shared his thoughts about a high-performance sedan with Chrysler division manager Ed Quinn. Quinn wanted something that would give Chrysler bragging rights on the Corvette and upcoming Thunderbird. Chrysler's success in the Mexican road race encouraged Quinn, as did Briggs Cunningham's Le Mans efforts and the Chrysler's NASCAR successes. The only way Chrysler could create a race car was to make the car from existing parts. Exner was brought in to discuss the look of the car. Cost limitations negated any redesign of the basic vehicle. Exner's partiality to the clean European lines led to a minimal amount of chrome, counter to the mid-1950s trend towards extra chrome. Exner determined that the new C-300, so named for the 300 horsepower Hemi engine under the hood, would only be produced in three colors: black, Platinum white, and Tango red.

Chrysler coined the term "forward look" to signal the adaptation of fighter-jet-like proportions and styling cues of the elegantly designed 1955 Chrysler cars. They covered the jet-intake-like headlight doors with chrome. In the rear, slender chrome tail fins stood proudly erect like a rudder on an F-86 Saber jet. Two V-8 powered models—the Windsor and the upscale New Yorker—comprised the basic 1955 Chrysler line. The Windsor had a single side spear while the New Yorker was given extra chrome, including a windshield eyebrow.

To create the C-300, designers fused the two-door, hardtop body of the Chrysler Windsor with the front clip from a 1955 Imperial. The stark simplicity of the C-300 contrasted sharply with the gaudy look of other Chrysler models. Designers positioned the number "300" in slanting chrome letters at the end of each side spear. The clean-shaven hood of the C-300 enhanced its simple lines. A special 300 emblem on a black and white checkerboard background nestled on the panel on the egg crate grille. Above this, simple chrome letters spelled out the name "Chrysler." Designers also placed the same checkerboard emblem on the deck lid the center of the 300's standard full wheel covers. To create these, they modified the wheel covers used on the Imperial with a new center insert. Buyers could purchase an optional set of chrome wire wheels. These wheels and the C-300's one-inch lower stance further enhanced the car's European look.

The interior trim of the New Yorker inspired the black and tan combination selected for the C-300. The C-300's leather front seat felt as comfortable as an expensive sofa. Designers continued the black and tan color scheme on the large steering wheel and instrument panel. The tan vinyl door and quarter trim panels complemented the black carpet. As was fitting for a race-bred car, the speedometer registered a maximum of 150 miles per hour, 30 miles per hour more than the standard Chrysler speedometer. Designers placed the chrome lever for the two-speed PowerFlite transmission to the right of the steering wheel on the instrument panel.

A Hemi lurked under the C-300's hood, its 300 horsepower eclipsing the V-8s of its competition. Cadillac's V-8 made 270 horsepower, Packard's 275, Lincoln's 225, and the Corvette's V-8 a mere 195. Like any Hemi engine, the 331-cubic-inch Chrysler Firepower liked to breathe so Chrysler added a dual Carter WCFB. The high-rise intake manifold required a delta-shaped air cleaner to clear the C-300's low sleek hood. Chrysler engineers increased the compression to 8.5:1 and added a longer duration solid lifter cam. The C-300 included dual exhaust with artfully crafted elliptically shaped chrome tips exiting beneath the rear bumper.

The 1957 Chrysler 300-C's low hood line required an inventive air-cleaner design for the large dual quad carburetors. The 300-C's standard Hemi engine produced 375 horsepower.

Chrysler delivered the new C-300s in time for the Daytona Speed Week competition. C-300s took first, second, and third in the American Stock Car Flying Mile competition with a top speed of 127.58 miles per hour. The C-300's early racing success was followed by many more victories in both the AAA and NASCAR series.

300-B

America's most powerful car got more powerful in 1956. Chrysler's engineers added a manual transmission option to satisfy the racers and new quarter panels featuring sleek fins to satisfy the general public. The 1956 300-B retained the same minimalist approach to exterior ornamentation, while providing maximum performance.

Exner's talented hand could be seen in the new rear treatment for the 1956 Chryslers. He reshaped the quarter panels to provide smooth sweeping lines. He integrated the taillights and rear bumper caps into the quarter panels, creating a unified look unlike that of the C-300, which had fins that looked like an afterthought. The tight integration of taillight, bumper, and quarter panel was a first for Chrysler, for whom the standard bumper arrangement was a simple beam with bumper and grille guards attached.

The rest of the 1956 300-B design changed very little from the 1955 C-300, with the exception of the shifter—pushbutton transmission controls mounted to the left of the steering wheel replaced the panel-mounted shift lever on the right. This slick feature created a real buzz among automotive journalists and the car-buying public.

Although the sleeker fins and pushbuttons were the most obvious change, Chrysler saved its trump card for the 300-B's engine, which pumped out an astounding 340 horsepower. Chrysler's engineers herded the additional ponies by increasing displacement to 354 ci and compression to

9:1. The Hemi now cranked out 35 more horsepower than Cadillac's V-8 and 115 more than the V-8 Corvette. The addition of the three-speed TorqueFlite automatic transmission appeared late in the production year.

Only one car satisfied the buyer looking for a stylish, fast car that cornered better than any passenger vehicle on the road—the Chrysler 300-B. But not everyone loved it. The 300-B suffered from the same pitfalls as any high performance vehicle: a harsh ride and an engine that required frequent maintenance. The unfortunate bank manager who upgraded from his cushy Buick Century quickly discovered the down-side of the stiff suspension and decided lope of the engine. The 300-B was not for someone looking for appliance-like transportation. Rather, it appealed to drivers who enjoyed the open road and didn't mind making a few sacrifices.

In 1957, AM radios were the best and only sound system available in a Chrysler 300-C.

The 1957 Chrysler 300-C featured unmatched styling and engineering. Virgil Exner created Chrysler's "Flight Sweep Styling" suite, with the 300-C as its centerpiece.

300-C

In 1957, Chrysler shocked the world with a completely redesigned car line. The Chrysler 300-C led the parade of stunning vehicles. Chrysler gambled that buyers would welcome drastic changes in its product line.

Once again the Chrysler 300-C had the distinction of being the most powerful car on the road, as well as one of the most beautiful. Available as either a convertible or hardtop, the 1957 300-C strutted clean lines which ran from crisp quad headlights to a pair of lofty tail fins. While designers added more chrome to other Chrysler models, they restricted the use of chrome on the 300-C to a thin quarter panel molding that ended in a round, tri-color 300-C emblem.

The 300-C's trapezoid-shaped grille featured an egg-crate pattern. Below the headlights, rectangular scoops fed cool air to the front brakes to reduce fade. The front bumper swept up at the ends and, in keeping with the clean design, had no bumper guards, unlike other Chrysler cars.

Like all 1957 Chrysler passenger cars, the 300-C rode on new front torsion bars. The 300-C featured 1.11-inch diameter bars rather than the standard 1.02-inch bars used on other models. These larger torsion bars increased the effective spring rate by 40 percent. The semi-elliptical rear spring leafs benefited from a 50-percent increase in spring rate over the standard rear springs.

The 1957 Chrysler was one of the first cars to integrate the front bumper into the overall design of the car's front end. The 1957 Chrysler was also one of the first cars to use quad headlights.

The forward lean of the front of the 1957 Chrysler 300-C gives the impression of speed and movement.

Throughout the 1950s, auto designers were heavily influenced by the design of jet aircraft. These aircraft were the inspiration for the sweeping fins of the time period.

The 1957 Chrysler 300-C's taillight and backup light were tightly integrated into one unpretentious fixture.

Chrysler's marketing managers eliminated wire wheels as an option. Chrysler then switched to 14-inch wheels to lower the car's profile and mounted special Goodyear Blue Streak whitewall tires. With an overall height of 54.7 inches, the 300-C had the lowest roofline of any Chrysler product in 1957. In addition to the three color choices, buyers could select a 300-C in Parade Green or Copper Brown. Those ordering a convertible had the choice of a black, green, blue or ivory convertible top.

Because of the car's lower profile, thin, less-comfortable, low-profile seats replaced the chair-height seats of the 1955 and 1956 models. Tan leather prevailed. The new instrument panel, with large circular pods housing gauges that rested in a deeply coved panel, looked as if it came out of an Air Force test plane.

In 1957, Chrysler upped the ante and increased the horsepower to a whopping 375. Displacement rose to 392 ci. Standard dual four-barrel carburetors, dual exhaust, and a long-duration camshaft expanded the Hemi's breathing power. Chrysler offered an optional racing package consisting of a 390-horsepower engine, SureGrip rear axle, low-restriction exhaust system, and three-speed manual transmission. But Chrysler's direct involvement in NASCAR racing diminished following the American Manufacturers Association's (AMA) 1957 racing ban.

Unbeatable performance and luxurious styling made the 300-C unique. It proved to be the best-selling letter car yet with a total of 2,251 delivered. It took a few years, but Chrysler had shaken off the shroud of stodgy styling and sprang years ahead. Chrysler matched the new exterior styling and increased power with improved ride and a more stable chassis. The 300-C owner's manual even advised buyers to handle its power with care.

300-D

The effect of the AMA's racing ban created a clear shift in the positioning of Chrysler's 1958 300-D. Chrysler's marketing team no longer touted the 300-D as a race-proven car; instead the car symbolized a lifestyle. But while the marketing department distanced itself from racing, engineers continued to refine the powerful Hemi engine.

The exterior of the 300-D changed little in 1958. This was due in large part to Virgil Exner's heart attack in 1956, when design work on the 1958 models was conducted. Designers changed the exterior by removing the windshield eyebrow molding. This cleaned up the front of the car and improved aerodynamics. Designers made the rear taillight lenses smaller and changed the hubcaps, which were inexpensive ways to alter the look of the vehicle. Similarly, they left the tall fins from

1957, because it would have been too costly to alter them. The 300-D offered six exterior colors: Raven Black, Aztec Turquoise, Mesa Tan, Tahitian Coral, Matador Red and Ermine White. Convertible tops came in ivory, green, blue or black. Designers stitched a new pattern into the tan leather seats, giving the impression of a four place seating arrangement.

In 1958, Chrysler produced the last first-generation Hemi engine. The 300-D carried a 392-ci Hemi, rated at 380 horsepower. Engineers raised the compression ratio to 10:1, but revised the camshaft for a smoother idle. In an effort to scoop Chevrolet and Pontiac, Chrysler offered an optional electronic fuel injection unit for the 300-D. Chrysler engineers had tinkered with this idea since 1954, which upped the horsepower to 390.

The few 300-Ds that were built with fuel injection had unique quarter panel emblems denoting the special equipment under the hood. For an additional $400, the buyer received a 40-amp generator, electric fuel pump and a fuel injection unit that used electric solenoids to meter fuel into the intake manifold. Chrysler later authorized the removal of these unreliable units and replaced them with the dual four-barrel setup.

300-E

Engineers worked under the hood to make big changes in the 1959 300-E. They introduced a new generation of wedge engine, thereby ending the Hemi's muscular reign. But Chrysler didn't emasculate the car completely. The less-expensive wedge engine still offered 380 horsepower—the level of performance expected by a 300 owner.

Designers attempted to give the 1959 300-E a facelift but failed to preserve the sleek lines of the earlier versions. They replaced the egg-crate grille with one featuring four slender horizontal bars.

The 1957 300-C's lower profile was enhanced with the addition of 14-inch-diameter wheels. This elegant black hardtop is fitted with a set of 15-inch-diameter chrome wire wheels. These were no longer an option in 1957, but could be purchased at the Chrysler parts counter.

The roomy rear seat of the
1957 Chrysler 300-C was also
covered in tan leather. The
elegant interior appointments
included bright transverse
headliner trim strips.

In addition to having a unitized body, the new 1957 Chryslers, like this 300-C hardtop, were fitted with smooth-riding torsion bar suspensions.

They added a simple chrome "300" emblem to the lower-left front corner of the hood and another emblem ahead of the rear wheel opening. They added a massive rear bumper and changed the taillights. To give the car a new look, designers added chrome molding to the rocker panel and to the rear wheel lip. These modifications had little merit in styling or practicality and did nothing to advance the clean lines of the C and D models.

Chrysler introduced some fancy gadgets to the interior of the 300-E. Standard swivel bucket seats rotated outward 40 degrees, allowing easier entry and exit. Designers covered the seats with "Living Leather." Engineers offered another gimmick that didn't work as well as expected: the True-Level Torsion-Aire suspension option. This automatic rear leveling system compensated for changes in ride height caused by variations in load weight.

Miserable sales of the 1959 300-E caused concern at Chrysler. Consumers purchased only 550 hardtops and 140 convertibles. Three factors drove customers away. The 300-E lost some of its sex appeal when the wedge replaced the Hemi, a cluttered look obscured the clean, sleek lines of earlier 300 models, and Chrysler failed to address some important quality-control issues from the 1957 300-C that persisted with the 300-E. To make matters worse, an economic recession resulted in a short supply of money, and consumers postponed the purchase of expensive vehicles. Thankfully, Chrysler didn't pull the plug on the 300.

300-F 1960

The Chrysler 300 survived and returned with a vengeance in 1960. Performance drove the design. Engineers designed a fully unitized body, installed a new ram induction system and offered an optional four-speed transmission.

The sleek Chrysler 300-F was the first of the third-generation Letter cars. Its unitized body offered an extremely rigid structure.

The fully restyled body of the 1960 Chrysler 300-F preserved the heritage of the beautiful 300-C. A broad bumper swept up at the ends. The front trapezoidal grille featured a single horizontal and vertical bar that crossed over a mesh background. A small red-white-and-blue 300 emblem rested at the intersection of these bars. Nine non-functional louvers graced the centerline at the rear of the hood.

The American public expected to see fins on a Chrysler car, and the 300-F delivered. The fins started at the center of the doors and swept back artfully to the new taillights. A thin chrome molding outlined the boomerang-shaped taillights. A faux spare tire clung to the center of the deck lid, like a bad toupee perched on the head of a cigar-chomping car salesman. Designers ran a chrome side spear from just behind the rear edge of the door to the top of the rear bumper and placed the 300-F emblem at its leading edge. Designers eliminated the extra chrome they had used on the 300-E.

Chrysler decided to use the "RB" 413-ci engine in the 300 for a second year. The performance of the new wedge engine confirmed its worth. In 1960, Chrysler offered two 413s: the base 375 horse-power and a high-performance 400 horsepower version, both with ram induction. This system included a pair of 30-inch manifolds with dual Carter AFB carburetors. The owner's manual stated, "The power plant of your 300-F introduces a unique principle in engine design for exhilarating performance ... the greatest advance since the supercharger."

Chrysler offered the optional 400 horsepower engine with a longer-duration solid-lifter cam. Chrysler engineers selected a French Pont-a-Mousson four-speed manual transmission—the same system that French engineers paired with the Chrysler-powered Facel Vega. The domestic version used

The classy 1960 Chrysler 300-F carried over many of the styling cues of the previous models. The standard engine was rated at 375 horsepower with an optional 400-horsepower engine available.

a cast iron case and required some reworking of the 300-F's transmission tunnel. Engineers mounted a tachometer, standard with the four-speed transmission, on the console, but drivers had difficulty reading it. Its inclusion was, however, a step in the right direction, since most drivers of high-performance vehicles wanted to know how far to push the engine.

Chrysler went back to basics with the 300-F. Designers cleaned up the styling and engineers introduced unibody construction to create a more rigid platform for the torsion bar suspension. Buyers returned to the showrooms in 1960 and boosted sales dramatically. Elegance and performance produced a winning combination.

Fins were still the rage in 1960 and Chrysler's 300-F fins were as bold as any ever installed on a Detroit-designed automobile.

300-G 1961

In 1961, General Motors and Ford Motor Company finally took note of what Chrysler had developed in the 300 series. A base 303 horsepower V-8 engine, with options up to 348 horsepower, powered Pontiac's luxurious Bonneville. Buyers could select engines up to 360 horsepower in Chevrolet's new high-performance Impala Super Sport. Both cars offered more trim and available four-speed transmissions. Over at Ford, the Mercury product planners worked on the Marauder, a sporty high-performance luxury car. Designers intended all of these cars to be distinctive and to have exceptional performance and handling qualities—traits bred into the 300 letter series models first developed in 1955.

Virgil Exner's reign as head of design ended in 1961. Flamboyant fins slowly disappeared. As stylish as they had been in 1957, fins received no fashion points by 1962. (Luckily for Chrysler, Cadillac failed to respond to changing trends in design and continued to sport fins, albeit smaller versions, than in previous years.) Designers inverted the traditional trapezoidal grille on the 300-G, turning it into a "smiling" grille instead of a "frowning" grille. This shape worked well with new canted quad headlights and upswept bumper ends. Rakish fins dominated the sculpted sides of the 300-G. Five ribs replaced the large circular mock spare tire on the deck lid. To combat the noise, vibration, and harshness that accompany a unitized body vehicle, Chrysler added 100 square feet of padding and sprayed 140 pounds of sound deadening compound into the body.

The same ram-inducted 375 horsepower 413-ci engine used in the 300-F powered the 300-G. The 400-horsepower version returned as an option. A three-speed transmission with a floor shift replaced the four-speed. Engineers included an alternator as standard equipment. It provided a better charging rate, weighed less, and was more durable than the generator it replaced. The return to 15-inch wheels improved brake cooling and reduced fade—a problem that plagued all 300s. In addition, the new full wheel covers featured ventilation slots to provide more air circulation around the brakes. Chrysler stepped up to the plate and provided the buyer

The 1960 Chrysler 300-F featured all-new styling and a unitized body. The base price for this elegant convertible was $5,841.

The faux spare tire stamped into the deck lid of the Chrysler 300-F completely disrupted an otherwise clean design.

In 1960, Chrysler offered an optional 400-horsepower engine for the 300-F, which could be equipped with a four-speed manual transmission.

with the best tires available—Goodyear 8.00X15 Blue Streak white walls. The interior remained virtually unchanged from 1960.

Even with a base price of $5,411 for the hardtop and $5,841 for the convertible, the 1961 Chrysler 300-Gs sold well. Its 375 horsepower engine had enough bravado for the highways and the refined styling, with the exception of the now outlandish fins, continued to turn heads. But even with the large fins, it respected and honored the heritage of the original Chrysler 300.

300-H 1962

Two things happened to the Chrysler 300 in 1962. Designers shaved off the tail fins and offered a non-letter version of the 300. The new design reflected an evolution in automotive styling trends that was long overdue. This change did not please Exner, whose role at Chrysler ended with this model.

To capitalize on the name recognition of the 300 and improve sales, Chrysler offered a less costly version of the model. These non-letter sporty cars replaced the Windsor line that was dropped in 1962. The new model sold exceptionally well at $2,000 less than the 300-H and featured optional bucket seats and a 305 horsepower engine. The standard 300 rolled on 14-inch wheels.

Engineers packaged several high-performance options into the 300-H. They upped the standard horsepower rating by 5, while eliminating ram induction. Engineers gave the 300-H a 413-ci engine with a dual four-barrel intake manifold that placed the carburetors in line. Chrysler boasted that the 380 horsepower engine in the 300-H "...was the most powerful standard engine in any American car." An optional engine included the ram induction system, hotter camshaft, and increased compression ratio for an advertised 405-horsepower rating. Chrysler offered an

aluminum-cased A427 Torqueflite as the standard transmission, with an optional three-speed manual transmission. The 300-H rolled on large, 7.60x15 tires with slotted wheel covers.

It was a tough year for Chrysler's seventh letter car. The 300-H lost its wings to a look-alike upstart that stole its sales. It would have been easy for Chrysler to pull the plug on the series, but Chrysler made the decision to stick with the letter cars for a few more years. The 1963s would have a new look and, possibly, an increase in sales.

300-J 1963

With the 1963 300-J, Chrysler created a much more conservative design than any of the previous 300 models. Designers added some chrome trim to the formal, sharp-edged 300-J, available only in a two-door hardtop model. They retained the trapezoidal grill shape, but placed the quad headlights on a horizontal plane. Designers gave the rear a clean look, dominated only by two large round tail-lights. Solid colors helped to preserve and enhance the upscale nature of the car.

The interior of the new 300-J featured a five-passenger seating capacity, with bucket seats up front and a bench in the rear. A full-length console split the front seats. Designers again used leather and chose the color "Claret" for the seats. The 300-J's unusual rectangular steering wheel gave the driver an excellent view of the instrument panel and easy entry and exit. However, drivers had difficulty spinning the rectangular steering in situations like parallel parking.

Chrysler offered only one engine on the 300-J—the ram-inducted, 390-horsepower 413. It was the only car in the Chrysler line to use the 413 engine with the longer, ram-induction manifolds. Engineers beefed up the standard TorqueFlite transmission, and offered a three-speed manual as an option.

In 1963, the 300-J listed for $5,177, while the standard 300 hardtop listed for $3,430. Chrysler also offered an optional 360 horsepower engine for the non-letter 300. A buyer could purchase a standard 300, add the optional 360hp engine, save $1,500, and congratulate himself on owning a standard 300 model with performance nearing the J model. Chrysler sold only four hundred 300-Js.

300-K 1964

Chrysler sales rebounded to record levels in 1964. The Chrysler 300-K, with sales of 3,647 units, helped drive this increase. This resurgence was due in a large part to a reduction in price. Chrysler brought back the convertible in 1964, but its sales were negligible (only 625 of the total 300-K production). The most obvious change to the exterior included the loss of the medallion in the center of the grille and use of a more geometric-shaped

In 1960, Chrysler canted the 300-F's fins at a slight outboard angle.

By 1960, the inverted trapezoid grille had become one of the highly identifiable features of a Chrysler. Chrysler designers placed a 300-F emblem at the center where the chrome bars crossed.

A long console ran from front to rear on the 1960 300-F. The front seats swiveled out to aid entry and exit.

taillight. Otherwise the body was the same as that of the 1963 model.

To reduce the cost of the 300-K, Chrysler removed many standard features. Designers replaced the leather interior with five shades of vinyl (leather was an option). They replaced the iconic 150 miles per hour speedometer with a standard, 120 miles per hour unit. Instead of using a few colors unique to the 300, designers relied on a broad palette of 17 exterior colors used for all Chrysler products.

Chrysler further reduced costs under the hood. Chrysler had always offered its most powerful engine as standard on the 300-model. With this model year engineers installed the less powerful 413-ci single four-barrel engine rated at 360 horsepower, though buyers could purchase a more powerful 390 horsepower engine as an option. The 390 featured ram induction manifolds and a higher compression ratio. Drivers shifted the standard TorqueFlite transmission using a console-mounted lever instead of pushbuttons.

Sales in 1964 of the 300-K model cramped the future of Chrysler's letter cars. The buying public no longer wanted a high-performance luxury car. Younger buyers wanted high performance, but not in a vehicle that looked like grandpa's. They wanted a Plymouth Fury or a Dodge Polara 500—cheap and fast. Chrysler understood this and began to phase out the 300 letter series.

300-L 1965

In 1965, Chrysler introduced the last in its series of 300 letter cars—the 300-L. Elwood Engle, Chrysler's new head of design, dramatically restyled the 300-L. Engle came from Ford and had a completely different design philosophy than his predecessor Virgil Exner. Engle created fresh and angular designs with long character lines highlighted by thin chrome strips. The concave sides of Engle's 300-L stood in sharp contrast to Exner's fins and curving shapes. The new 300-L looked much longer than the 300-K, due to an abundance of horizontal lines. Designers added tempered glass headlight shields unique to the 300-L. They placed a running light in the center of the grille, but since this was illegal in some states, many owners disconnected them.

Engineers offered only one engine for the 1965 300-L model: a 360-horsepower, 413-ci V-8. They installed a TorqueFlite with console-mounted shifter as the standard transmission, and offered a four-speed manual transmission as a no-cost option. The 300-L had few of the dramatic elements found in earlier 300 letter cars. They bowed out quietly as Chrysler's Super Stock and NASCAR efforts took center stage.

The early Chrysler 300 letter cars broke new ground in the automotive world. They bucked the mid-1950s design trends of too much chrome and too many colors. Their minimalist styling proved that less was more. They proved that a full-size passenger car could have sports car characteristics. The 300s also established the formula for early 1960s muscle cars—big engines with a sleek, no-frills, full-size body. Chrysler returned to this formula in 1968 with the Road Runner. Chrysler's constant development of the Hemi engine provided new tools for the marketing staff and high-performance driving pleasure for the buyers. When the Hemi faded from view, a powerful new series of wedge engines was added, picking up where the Hemi left off. Although built in limited numbers—over the 11-year lifespan, Chrysler built only 16,857 units—the Chrysler 300s represent an important part of the history of the muscle car era.

This white 1957 Chrysler 300-C is parked in the driveway of the Palm Springs, California house formerly owned by Frank Sinatra.

chapter two

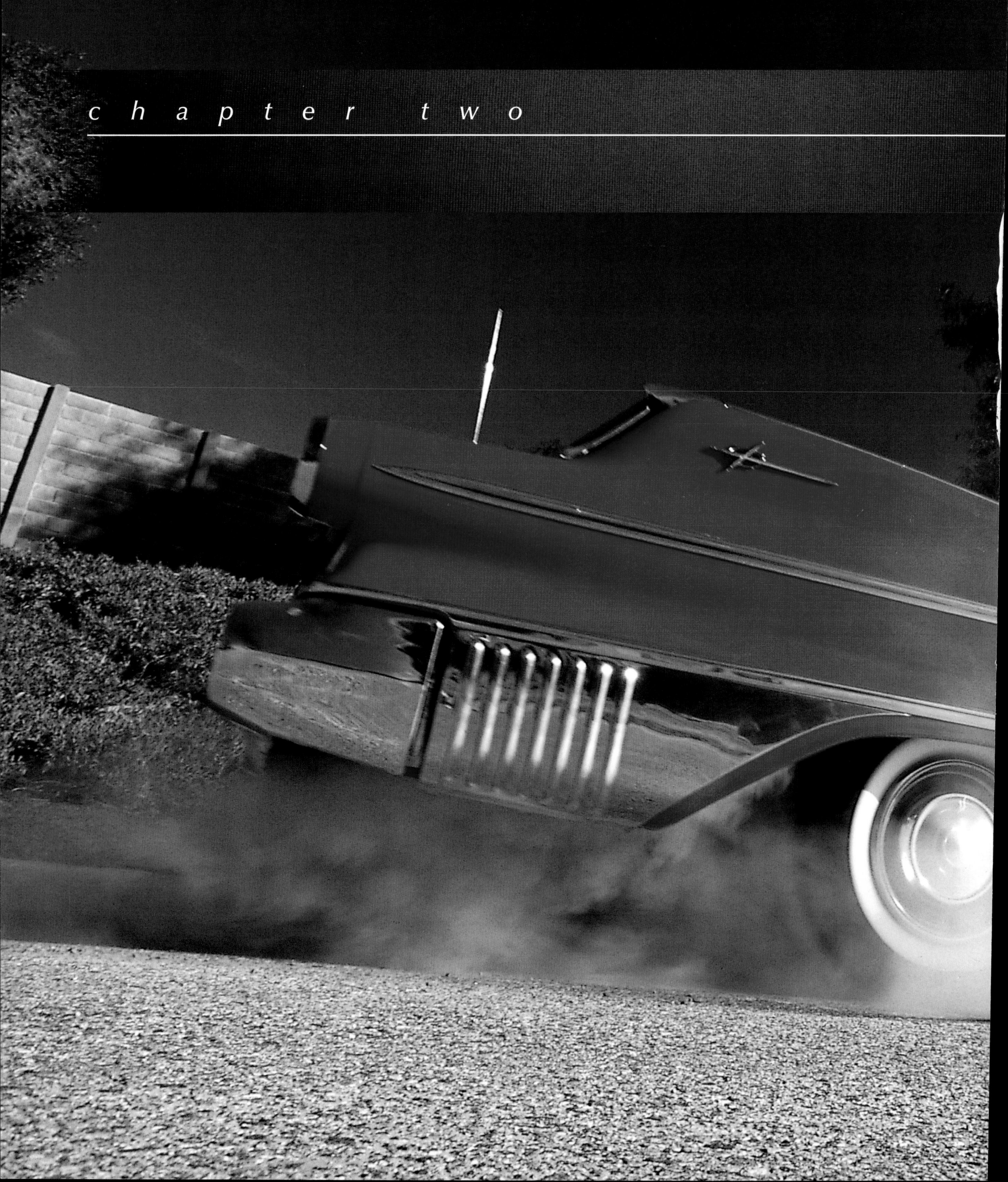

(previous) The D-500's powerful 383 engine can easily turn white sidewall tires into clouds of white smoke.

The 1960 Dodge's oval-shaped steering wheel provided the driver with more leg room and a clear sightline to the speedometer.

MOPAR'S DODGE AND PLYMOUTH PERFORMANCE CARS OF THE 1950s

The 1950s were a dynamic time to be working in the auto industry and to be living in Detroit. Although the war put the auto industry on hold and recovery had taken ten long years, by 1955 automotive design had finally caught up and engineering advances that had been lost during the war years were reclaimed. The auto industry had learned a great deal from making weapons systems during the war and many of these technical advances were adapted to the latest generation of Detroit Iron. The use of color also played an important role in the fresh look of the automobiles of the 50s. New colors and two- and three-tone paint schemes highlighted automotive design that mimicked the shape of high-speed flight. The last half of the decade was going to be dramatic, especially for Chrysler.

In the early 1950s, product evolution at Chrysler churned around the emerging V-8 engine. Chrysler's development of its 1955 C-300 into a 300 horsepower powerhouse wasn't lost on other divisions. Dodge and DeSoto had been nursing their smaller-displacement Hemi engines along in the shadow of the larger Chrysler firepower. Plymouth was the only Chrysler division without a Hemi engine, but engineers developed a unique polyspherical V-8 that was improved to match the competition for sales dollars on the racetrack and at the dealerships. The C-300 was one of the best things that happened for other Chrysler divisions. Dodge and Plymouth eventually developed cars with unique personalities and performance packages that mimicked the bold Chrysler letter cars.

The 1956 DeSoto Pacesetter convertible was powered by a 330-ci Fireflite Hemi engine that developed 255 horsepower. While an appealing performance car, it was not enough to save Chrysler's DeSoto division. The DeSoto brand was consigned to the history books by the time the muscle car wars began in earnest in the 1960s.

(below) In 1956, DeSoto created a special Pacesetter convertible by adding the gold trim from the Adventurer model. A DeSoto Pacesetter convertible, similar to this one, paced 33 cars to the start of the 1956 Indianapolis 500.

Dodge introduced its Red Ram Hemi engine in 1953. In 1954, Dodge President William Newberg drove a yellow, Hemi-powered Dodge convertible as pace car for the Indianapolis 500—the first Dodge to ever pace the 500. To commemorate the event, Dodge offered a mid-year package called the Royal 500, a special trim package added to the new Royal convertible. This package included a special crossed checkered flag emblem for the deck lid and front fenders, as well as the addition of a chrome "500" emblem on the quarter panel. In addition, a large continental kit hung off the rear. The pace car rolled on chrome wire wheels, also part of the factory Royal 500 package. Officially, Dodge built 701 of these pace car replicas and undoubtedly, enterprising dealers converted many more standard Royal convertibles into Royal 500s.

The basic Red Ram 241-ci Hemi for 1954 delivered 150 horsepower. Dodge dealers stocked an Offenhauser intake manifold and four-barrel carburetor that could be added for an additional $87. No horsepower figures were given for this option. Though the design of the 1954 Dodge was brutally outdated, the 500 package was a good start for Dodge performance vehicles.

By 1955, Chrysler engineers had increased the Red Ram's horsepower to 193 with the addition of a factory four-barrel carburetor in the top-of-the-line Royal Lancer. Designers had also signifi-

In 1956, Plymouth introduced its Fury high-performance sport coupe. All Sport Furys produced that year were painted off-white and fitted with special gold trim and hubcaps.

When first introduced, the 1957 Dodge was on the very sharp leading edge of automobile design.

(below) The 1956 Sport Fury was based on the Belvedere. Plymouth used gold anodized aluminum for the Fury's bold side molding.

cantly improved the styling of the 1955 Dodge. Virgil Exner's forward look design philosophy had produced the longest, lowest, widest, and most sporty Dodge cars ever. They featured wrap-around windshields, plenty of chrome, and three-tone paint schemes. Designers placed a large chromed "V" on the front hood of those equipped with a V-8 engine. Although the new Dodge didn't have fins like so many of its contemporaries, it sported taillights that looked like miniature jet exhausts. Dodge failed to capitalize on the success of the previous year's Royal 500 package. Instead, Dodge executives stood on the sidelines of the clean lines and high-performance engine of the 1955 Chrysler C-300. Dodge and Plymouth would finally get the picture in 1956.

In 1956, all the major automotive manufacturers offered overhead-valve V-8 engines. Even the lowly transportation cars like Chevrolet, Ford, and Plymouth

offered powerful and fuel-efficient V-8s. The manufacturers of these cars looked for ways to improve the horsepower of their basic V-8s. They wanted to transform ordinary cars into special vehicles with glitz and glamour to match their growing horsepower.

The success of the 1955 Chrysler C-300 provided the business model for Dodge and Plymouth in 1956. Dodge jumped into the performance sedan arena with its D-500, an engine-chassis package. This option was available for any of the new 1956 Dodge body styles but it fit best into the sleek hardtops and convertibles. The D-500 option included the 315 cubic-inch Red Ram Hemi engine rated at 260 horsepower. To achieve this power, Dodge added a longer-duration cam (252 degrees), high-compression pistons, and dual exhaust. Dodge added a heavier frame, heavy-duty springs, and 12-inch Chrysler brakes to cars equipped with the D-500 option. The California Highway Patrol was so impressed with the performance of the new Dodge that they ordered 200 vehicles with the D-500 option to be used on patrol duty. This was Chrysler's first move into the world of specialized law-enforcement vehicles, territory that Ford had claimed for years. The success of the Dodge D-500 option spawned decades of special police packages and additional fleet sales for Chrysler.

In 1956, Dodge offered a D-500-1 designed strictly for racing. Engineers added a 280-degree-duration cam and dual four-barrel carburetors for 295 horsepower. The D-500-1 option was available only in a Coronet hardtop, convertible, or two-door sedan with a manual transmission. Dodge used the D-500-1 to set several speed records on the sand at Daytona and on the salt flats of Bonneville. Engineers designed these special cars for NASCAR events (NASCAR had a convertible class) and drag racing competition.

In 1957, the D-500 option included a 285-horsepower 325-ci Red Ram Hemi engine. Dodge also offered a Super D-500 rated at 285 horsepower. Both included dual exhaust with slick oval-shaped chrome tips.

Tail fins dominated all of Chrysler's offerings for the 1956 model year, including the new Dodge. Engineers gave the 1955 model a facelift to create the basic car for 1956. Tall tail fins enhanced the rear of the new Dodge. The body side trim gently swept down toward the rear bumper as it crossed the quarter panel and then abruptly angled up to meet the top edge of the fin in front of the taillight. This new trim scheme provided hard break lines for the popular tri-tone paint schemes. A small crossed-flag emblem, fitted to the right side of the deck lid and the left front of the hood, identified the Dodge D-500 option.

Spinster librarians and grandparents had traditionally represented Plymouth's target market. Plymouths generally lacked style and consistently lacked power. Designers and engineers had created an uncomplicated design that promised long and faithful service, like an old hound dog. But things changed in 1955. The change sprang from the tip of Virgil Exner's pencil, where stylish sweeping lines replaced stodgy, square-edged ones. Chrysler's "Forward Look" campaign filtered down to its lowest-priced sedan—a move that turned the frog into a prince. The new 1955 Plymouth featured clean lines and a front end that leaned forward, giving the impression that the car was moving forward even while standing still. Tastefully designed rear fins matched the look of the car's front-end design. It was a well-balanced execution that took a few cues from the aircraft industry and was easily the equal of its contemporaries. In addition, it offered an optional V-8 that placed it in the same league as those low-priced cars with their fresh, overhead-valve V-8s. The new Plymouth took advantage of everything that was happening within Chrysler and Dodge and distinguished itself from the competition.

Fins came to America with a flourish in 1956. Chrysler's vehicles, designed by Virgil Exner, were leading the parade. When Plymouth introduced its new 1956 model line on October 21, 1955, it had fins. With a forward-leaning nose and tall tail fins, the car looked like an Air Force F-86 Saber jet on wheels. On January 7, 1956, Plymouth spiced up the recipe by introducing a new top-of-the-line model known as the Fury. (Interestingly, the Fury was the U.S. Navy's version of the F-86 Saber.) The Plymouth Fury was a special high-performance coupe based on the Belvedere, Plymouth's 1956 model carrying its highest level of trim. All 1956 Plymouth Fury models were two-door hardtops painted a solid Egg Shell white. The Fury's bold side trim highlighted the car's dramatic profile. Plymouth added a large, tapered, gold-anodized panel on the sides surrounded by thin, chromed strips. This insert panel ran from the front fender to the rear of the car, with an abrupt step up at the rear that accentuated the bold tail fins. Designers placed a special Fury emblem within the gold insert on the quarter panel. They also used the gold tone on the Fury's grille and special full wheel covers. This extensive use of gold-anodized trim was a first for the industry.

Chrysler's penchant for building an entire performance package extended to the Plymouth Fury. Instead of just punching up Plymouth's existing 277-ci, polyspherical V-8 engine, engineers borrowed a 303-ci, polyspherical engine used in the Canadian Chrysler Windsor and Dodge Royal models. With a 9.25:1 compression ratio and single four-barrel carburetor, this engine developed healthy power. A hot solid-lifter camshaft, heavy-duty valve springs, and dual exhausts helped the

In 1957, the D-500 option included a 285-horsepower 325-ci Red Ram Hemi engine. Dodge also offered a Super D-500 rated at 310 horsepower. Both included dual exhaust with slick oval-shaped chrome tips.

In 1959, the Dodge received a distinctive set of cat's-eye headlight brows. There were two 383-ci D-500 engines in 1959, one rated at 320 horsepower and the other rated at 345 horsepower.

Jet aircraft–inspired styling dominated automobile design in the late 1950s. This 1959 Dodge taillight resembles the tail of a 1950s-era jet fighter.

In 1959, the Custom Royal was Dodge's top model. This chrome piece was at the leading edge of the tail fin.

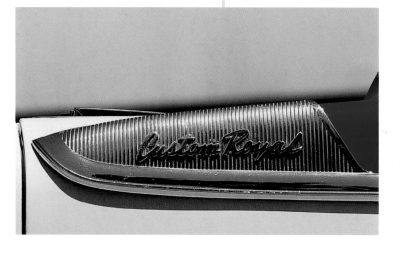

engine reach 240 horsepower. Either a three-speed manual transmission or a pushbutton-operated PowerFlite automatic backed this engine, the only one available in the Fury. Heavy-duty springs and larger 7.10x15 tires (all other 1956 Plymouths rode on 6.70x15s) on 5 1/2 inch wide wheels gave the 1956 Plymouth Fury superior handling. The Fury's special interior featured bench seats with off-white vinyl bolsters and a black and white simulated brocade insert, highlighted with golden threads. The Fury also had a standard feature no other American performance sedan would have for years: a tachometer. Designers placed the Stewart-Warner tachometer on the instrument panel to the right of the speedometer where it could be easily seen.

With the introduction of the 383 "B" wedge engine, the Hemi engine was no longer part of Dodge's performance equation in 1959. The D-500 single four-barrel version produced 320 horsepower and the dual-quad Super D-500 produced 345 horsepower.

The fins on the 1960 Dodge were subdued. This was a time when the other carmakers sprouted large fins to catch up to the trend that Chrysler started years earlier.

The 1960 Dodge Matador rode on a long 122-inch wheelbase chassis.

Plymouth finally appeared on the performance map. By the end of 1956, 4,485 Plymouth Fury models had been sold and a new performance car had been born.

The staggering advancements in styling and engine technology Chrysler made in the mid-1950s continued into 1957, a record year for progress on both fronts. Some of Virgil Exner's finest work was the 1957 Dodge and Plymouth offerings.

The dynamic new 1957 Plymouth was lower, wider, and looked longer than the 1956 model. It also sprouted the highest tail fins of any production car to date. The evolution of the 1957 Plymouth was a revolution with outstanding results.

Plymouth engineers designed a new frame for the 1957 model. They lengthened the wheelbase by 3 inches and added torsion-bar suspension to the front. In addition to providing an excellent ride, the use of a torsion bar front had the advantage of lowering the car more than traditional coil springs could. This design, in combination with the addition of 14-inch wheels, resulted in a car that was about two inches lower than the 1956 model, and almost 4-inches wider.

Previously, Plymouth's two-door hardtop looked more like a sedan without B-pillars. The 1957 Plymouth hardtop had been specifically designed as a hardtop. In the past, four-door sedans had been Plymouth's featured vehicles. Now the sleek new Belvedere hardtop and convertible would

The Dodge matador was the base full-size Dodge model in 1960. The Matador script was placed on the front fender.

lead the Plymouth parade. Spinsters and librarians had to look elsewhere for their no-frills cars.

The dynamic Fury returned in 1957 at the top of Plymouth's stylish lineup. Like 1956, the Fury was available only as a two-door hardtop. Designers chose Sand Dune White for the exterior color and a cocoa-and-beige interior accented with gold-flecked trim. Although engineers dropped the tachometer for the 1957 Fury package, they added a 150-mile-per-hour speedometer to the stylish instrument panel. The full-length, hockey stick-shaped, gold-anodized side trim worked well with Plymouth's svelte new body. Designers added gold tones to the Fury's expansive grille and full wheel covers. Heavy-duty springs and 14x6-inch wheels completed the equation. The sporty 1957 Fury clearly improved upon the design concepts and engineering of the 1956 model.

Under the hood both Dodge and Plymouth enjoyed added performance in the best Mopar tradition. In 1957, engineers bored Plymouth's 277 ci V-8 to create a strong running 301 ci engine. With a two-barrel carburetor, they rated this engine at 215 horsepower and called it the "Fury 301." When engineers added a four-barrel carburetor, the horsepower jumped to 235 and the name was changed to the "Fury 301 Quad." While the Fury name was used on the 301 ci V-8, the engines were never installed in a 1957 Fury. The true Fury engine for 1957, called the "Fury V-800," displaced 318 ci and was a stroked version of the 301. With a compression ratio of 9.25:1, a hot solid lifter cam, and dual quads, this polyspherical engine produced 290 horsepower. Plymouth offered this engine as standard equipment on the Fury, and as an option on other 1957 models. A three-speed, column-shifted manual transmission served as the standard gearbox. Plymouth offered for the first time the new TorqueFlite three-speed automatic transmission with push button control, a vast improvement over the old PowerFlite automatic.

In addition to being one of the most powerful cars on the road, the 1960 Dodge Polara was one of the most elegant.

The 1957 Dodge line of automobiles also benefited from Exner's keen eye and artistic hand. Like the 1957 Plymouth, the Dodge made a quantum leap in styling with extraordinary rear fins positioned on a lower, sleeker body. But unlike Plymouth, Dodge's special D-500 performance option was no longer a sporty package combining performance-based, heavy-duty components and exterior badges. For 1957, the D-500 boiled down to a $72 option that included heavy-duty suspension and a larger engine. The D-500 option included a 325 cubic-inch Red Ram Hemi engine that produced 285 horsepower. Dodge offered a three-speed manual transmission as standard equipment, with the TorqueFlite automatic as a $220 option. In 1957, buyers could choose an optional dual four-barrel equipped D-500 325 ci Red Ram Hemi engine that produced 310 horsepower.

The D-500 engine offered plenty of horsepower to move this heavy 1960 Dodge Polara convertible down the road.

In 1957, Dodge and Plymouth built on the success of the 1956 D-500 and Fury models. Both brands would use the performance gains they had made in 1956. This extra power, combined with dramatic new styling and a sophisticated Torsionaire suspension, helped drive a jump in sales. Because of its excellent exterior and engine package, Plymouth fared best in the performance world of 1957, selling 7,438 Fury models, many with the D-500 package.

In 1958, Chrysler increased the horsepower in the Plymouths and Dodges, but production numbers fell due to a recession. Selling any car with expensive options during a recession became nearly impossible. The cars built by Plymouth and Dodge in 1956 and 1957 also hurt new car sales. They were rife with flaws in quality that continued to haunt them in 1958. Chrysler's engineering staff persevered. Dodge designed a new engine to replace the Hemi and Plymouth upgraded its polyspherical V-8. Even though sales were down, Plymouth and Dodge saw a future with more horsepower.

The 1958 Plymouth received a mild facelift consisting of quad headlights, a new lower front valence panel, revised side trim, and new taillights. The Fury returned as a special Belvedere model, available only as a two-door hardtop. For 1958, Plymouth abandoned the white exterior paint color that had covered the 1956 and 1957 Fury model, in favor of the creamy Buckskin Beige. Designers retained the Fury's now signature hockey stick-shaped gold side trim, grille, and wheel covers. The

use of anodized side trim and golden highlighted emblems on the Fury filtered down to other Plymouth models. Designers added a gold "V" emblem to the grille of every 1958 Plymouth equipped with a V-8 engine. A silver-anodized "Sportone" side trim was optional on the Belvedere and Sport Suburban. This gave the Belvedere or Sport Suburban buyer an opportunity to purchase a vehicle with the panache of a Fury at a lower price.

The 1958 Fury continued to be one of the most distinctive cars on the road. In addition to the gold trim, each Fury also featured heavy-duty suspension, bumper wing guards, standard backup lamps,

A complete redesign of the 1960 Dodge resulted in the removal of the cat's-eye headlight eyebrows for more traditionally styled headlight bezels.

The cars of the 1960s were covered with fine details such as this slender die casting at the end of the tail fins that housed a red reflector on the 1960 Dodge.

and dual exterior mirrors. The interior of the Fury remained tasteful, wrapped in Buckskin Beige and Cocoa with gold highlights, a two-tone steering wheel, and a 150-mile-per-hour speedometer.

Subtle changes to the exterior of the 1958 Plymouth revealed little of the changes under the hood. The Fury still held sway with the most powerful standard engine, the dual-quad, 318-cubic-inch engine rated at 290 horsepower. But there was also a completely new optional engine with even more power: the 350 cubic-inch "B" engine. Chrysler's B engine is distinguished by its deep skirt block design and front-mounted distributor. This new B engine, named the "Golden Commando," developed 305 horsepower. With the B engine, Chrysler engineers created a true wedge, not another polyspherical or Hemi engine. This engine proved to have long legs and would stand the test of time as one of Chrysler's best engine designs. Plymouth also offered a short-lived, Bendix-built electronic fuel injection unit that boosted horsepower on the Golden Commando engine to 315, but at $500 for an extra 10 horsepower, it was a costly option. Because of the failure rate of this new fuel injection system, they were all recalled and replaced with dual quads.

In 1958, Plymouth fought for recognition in the low-priced performance segment of the market. Chevrolet and Pontiac both offered tri-power carburetion and fuel injection on their 1958 cars; Plymouth had to stay in the race with its new B engine and a new fuel injection system. Each manufacturer was adding catchy names to their performance engines. Plymouth kept up with its Golden Commando (for the new 350 ci engine), "Dual Fury" (for those 318 cubic-inch V-8s equipped with dual quads), and "Power Pack" (for any single four-barrel equipped V-8).

In 1958, Dodge had low sales due to the recession, as did other auto manufacturers. Dodge also failed to take advantage of the success of the sporty Plymouth Fury and Chrysler 300, again only offering an uncomplicated design without many extras. This may have been due to the positioning of the Dodge against Buick, Oldsmobile, and Mercury, none of which had a sporty model. Like Plymouth, only a light facelift was given to the stylish and well-accepted Dodge "Flight Sweep" look.

Dodge's 1960 D-500 engine developed 320 horsepower with the help of these cross ram intake manifolds and dual Carter AFB carburetors.

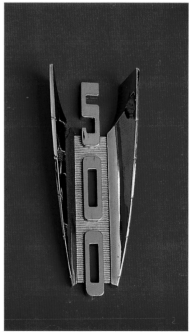

The discrete D-500 ornamentation on the 1960 Dodge gave little hint of the power under the hood.

The Flight Swept look of the 1957 Dodge stopped people in their tracks and caused a buzz within the automotive world. But this brought higher expectations for the 1958 model, which proved to be a disappointment for many. The 1958 model got a facelift that took away some of the purity of the 1957.

Engines were the biggest news for Dodge in 1958. Three V-8s were on the option list and only the 325 cubic-inch engine was a carryover. Like Plymouth, Dodge saw the extended virtue of the soon-to-be-corporate "B" block and used two versions, one displacing 350 ci and the other 361. Both the 1958 Dodge and the Plymouth Fury used the same 350 cubic-inch B block base engine.

Chrysler designers boldly experimented with gauge and control placement throughout the late 1950s and early 1960s, as evidenced by the innovative speedometer on this 1960 Dodge.

Instead of dual quads, Dodge used a single four-barrel carburetor and rated it at 295 horsepower. A .060 overbore of the 350 created the additional 6 ci in the Dodge 361 B engine. The D-500 option added one of the 361 ci engines: a 305-horsepower model equipped with a single four-barrel carburetor, a 320-horsepower model with dual quads, or a 333-horsepower version fitted with Bendix fuel injection. Unfortunately, the Bendix fuel injection failed as miserably on the Dodge D-500 as it had on the Plymouth Fury.

In the early 1950s, juggling engine displacements under the Chrysler banner proved costly, but justifiable in light of the fact that each model had its own specific V-8 engine. All General Motors cars of the era were fitted with uniquely designed engines that were not interchangeable; a Cadillac V-8 would not interchange with a Buick, and an Oldsmobile would not interchange with a Chevy. It was a brilliant marketing concept, but expensive. Designing a "corporate" engine was the most cost-effective thing to do, but in the early 1950s would have been marketing suicide. When Chrysler introduced the new B engine in 1957, it lacked the funds to offer an exclusive wedge engine for each car line as it had done with the Hemi. They offered the same basic B engine with slightly different displacements, essentially to fool the car buyers. In reality, Chrysler was ahead of its time when it decided to build a single, high-quality, large-displacement engine for all of its car lines.

Chrysler was on a technological roll in 1958. Engineers introduced a powerful new "B" wedge engine and ventured into the minefield of fuel injection. Unfortunately, they got their legs blown off at the knees. Releasing such an expensive option during a recession year proved to be poor timing. The system hadn't been as thoroughly tested as had the Rochester mechanical fuel injection system Chevrolet installed on the Corvette. Chrysler's Bendix fuel injection system proved to be the "Airflow"

of fuel management systems. Had they stuck with it, Chrysler might have revolutionized the internal combustion engine the way refined electronic fuel injection systems did in the mid-1980s. They did the smartest thing they could at the time and abandoned designing a better fuel injection system.

There were some positive events in 1958. Chrysler celebrated the assembly of its 25-millionth car. The government approved an additional $1.8 billion to speed up the construction of the interstate highway system. The expansion of this vast highway system, coupled with inexpensive gasoline, encouraged the public to buy cars worthy of extended road trips. This raised Chrysler's confidence to build a wide spectrum of large cars with powerful engines.

The year 1959 will go down in history as the year that the American auto industry took leave of its senses and built outrageous cars with exceptionally large fins. The first, and loudest, shot of the fin wars of 1959 came from Chevrolet, followed by a strong volley from the other GM models. But as GM tried to catch up to Chrysler's sleek-finned offerings, Chrysler was planning to abandon tail fins and revise completely the way its cars were constructed. Technology led the way for Chrysler's offerings in 1959, though fins were not forgotten.

Plymouth restructured its 1959 lineup of cars by eliminating the low-end Plaza model and downgrading the Savoy and the Belvedere. The Fury became a separate series with a convertible,

Though outrageous by today's standards, the tail fins of the 1960 Dodge were relatively subdued compared to other cars of the period.

The "Forward Look" design theme continued into 1960 on the Dodge with the aggressive lean of its headlamp bezels.

two hardtops, and a four-door sedan. The Sport Fury replaced the Fury as Plymouth's performance car. Plymouth's top-of-the-line car could be purchased as either a hardtop or a convertible, but the distinctive gold trim was missing.

In the automobile business, annual changes often consist of nothing more than a facelift of an existing model. The manufacturer enjoys significant cost savings by not having to completely retool its plant. The annual facelift often produces an acceptable product, but one that is not significantly better than the original. And sometimes, as was the case with the 1959 Plymouth, a facelift produces a car that's decidedly less attractive than the original.

Plymouth took the clean, classic lines of the 1957 and 1958 models and "busied" them up. In the front, designers gave the eyebrow over the headlights a depression between the lights, and enlarged the grid of the anodized grille. They increased the flair of the tail fins, and the neatly integrated taillight of the 1957 and 1958 Plymouths gave way to bizarre add-ons. The biggest add-on of all was the "Flight Sweep" deck lid on the Fury two-door hardtop and convertible models. This fake rear tire looked like a giant Frisbee resting on the deck lid. It was simply bolted on and didn't blend well with the car's overall design. (This mock rear tire, Exner's homage to the classic European cars, would reappear on the 1960 Chrysler 300-F.) Indeed, 1959 was an outrageous year for automobile design.

In 1959, Plymouth subtly moved from the jet-aircraft era into the space age. Designers added a large, circular, chrome emblem to the Fury's quarter panel. Inside this emblem they placed a rocket poised for vertical flight. It was no coincidence that the U.S. government launched its Jupiter ballistic missile in 1959, and that the Chrysler Corporation built the missile.

In 1959, Plymouth continued to refine its under-hood offerings. The Sport Fury's standard V-8, named the V-800, displaced 318 ci and developed 260 horsepower. For an extra $74, the optional 361 cubic inch, 305-horsepower Golden Commando engine could be added. This engine, also known as the "Golden Commando 395" for the 395 ft-lb of torque it produced, was an option in all of the other 1959 Plymouth models except the lowly Savoy.

Many features on the 1959 Plymouth could be defined as novelties. The list included swivel front seats, an automatic-tilt rear view mirror, Instant Air gas heater, Constant Level air suspension, and padded steering wheel. It was painful to see such items added to a basic transportation car when two years earlier, the Plymouth had been heralded as a trend-setter and acclaimed for its torsion-bar suspension. When gimmicks—instead of solid styling and expert engineering—define a car, it's a clear sign of trouble. This was proven in 1959 when Plymouth's market share dropped 13 percent.

Dodge also received a minor facelift in 1959 with better results than Plymouth's. Designers added chrome eyebrows over the headlights, giving the front end a sinister scowl. They reshaped its lengthy tail fins, which remained as bold as ever. Overall, the new Dodge retained its strong, highly identifiable lines. Dodge did fall prey to the inclusion of widgets—swing-out seats, automatic headlight beam changers, and a raft of other thingamabobs that didn't improve the overall vehicle.

Fortunately, Dodge retained and improved the D-500 option. They bored the B block to 4.25 inches and created the 383, an engine that would gain legendary status among Mopar owners. The base D-500 engine was equipped with a single four-barrel carburetor and produced 320 horsepower. The Super D-500 raised the horsepower to 345 with twin Carter AFB carburetors. Both engines were expensive, ranging between $300 and $400, but that price included the TorqueFlite automatic transmission. Other than the small "500" emblem on the fins, the only indication that a 1959 Dodge was equipped with the D-500 option was the roar from the dual chrome exhaust tips and the cloud of dust left hanging in the air as the sleek Dodge sped away.

In 1960, Chrysler revolutionized the way it built cars. Chrysler's long tradition of building cars with body-on-frame construction was shelved for a fully unitized body. A unitized automobile body is constructed from a number of internal and external panels that are welded into a single structural element strong enough to eliminate the need for a traditional frame. This is similar to the monocoque construction of aircraft and Formula 1 race cars that do not have a distinctive single frame. Unitized bodies are less expensive to build and are much more rigid than body-on-frame vehicles. The biggest problem with a unitized body is the road noise and vibration transmitted through the body structure. Chrysler's superb staff faced this challenge and engineered the structural integrity needed while minimizing the negative side effects.

The change to a unitized body required changes to the external styling as well. The styling of Chrysler's vehicles had first been introduced in 1957 and it was time for a new look. As advanced as Chrysler's products were at their debut, they still had to be restyled to stay ahead of the competition.

The 1960 Dodge Matador and Polara featured abbreviated tail fins and a single round taillight.

The optional "Music Master" radio (AM only) cost an additional $59 on a 1960 Dodge.

(below) Modern space-age graphics were used on the center of the 1960 Dodge steering wheel.

Technology was changing rapidly in the 1950s. Although Chrysler had been three years ahead of the competition with its cars in 1957, the car-buying public expected more and more each year. With the redesign of 1960 models, Dodge and Plymouth got what they needed with respect to styling.

Plymouth's styling for 1960 saw a rebirth of clean, well-integrated lines with bold fins. The new 1960 Dodge also featured cleaner styling and reshaped fins, which were more subdued than in previous years. On hardtop models, the fins started at the rear edge of the door opening and on sedans, they began at the C-pillar.

From a marketing standpoint, Plymouth and Dodge positioned their new 1960s models differently than they had in the past. In the late 1950s, performance was at the forefront, as evidenced by the showcasing of the sporty Fury and D-500 options. Now strength, reliability, and economy were highlighted. This was an unusual position for Dodge, which had been in the same class as Oldsmobile and Mercury—the new Dodge Dart model was now being compared to a Ford or Chevy. The Dodge ads featured the economy of its new six-cylinder engine, while Plymouth's ads featured the car's structural integrity and anticipated longevity.

Plymouth was fighting a losing battle against Rambler and also had to compete with its sister division for sales in its own

Chrysler was heavily involved with America's space program in 1960. This involvement was exemplified by the new Jetson-styled ornamentation on the 1960 Dodge's tail fin.

market segment. The Sport Fury was dropped for 1960 to emphasize economy. The Fury continued as the top-of-the-line model, but its standard engine was a 101 horsepower six.

Even though both Dodge and Plymouth downplayed performance, each offered a good selection of powerful engines, starting with the 361 ci V-8 rated at 305 horsepower installed in both models. Dodge called it the "Ram Fire V-8," and Plymouth called it the "Golden Commando." Plymouth added the long ram intake manifolds to the 361 to create the 310-horsepower "Sonoramic Commando" engine. Dodge offered the D-500 option again in 1960, with a standard, single-four-barrel-equipped 383 ci engine rated at 320 horsepower. Plymouth offered the same 383-engine (without a catchy name) rated at 325 horsepower. Plymouth's ram-inducted 383 was rated at 330 horsepower and also called the "Sonoramic Commando." Dodge called its ram inducted 383-engine the "Super D-500," rated at 345 horsepower.

Both Plymouth and Dodge received a major facelift in 1961, but Exner's styling efforts missed the mark. Plymouth lost its fins and Dodge's fins were reduced in size and reversed. Instead of leading design trends, the cars were now out of sync with the mainstream GM and Ford products. The fickle public rejected the new cars. Plymouth placed seventh in sales—a long fall from the third-place position held a few years earlier. Dodge sales dropped 25 percent in 1961. The fact that Dodge and Plymouth still offered high performance engines was not enough to save them in a market where customers also wanted good-looking cars. Dodge once again offered the D-500 option, the most powerful being a 375 horsepower 413 ci "RB" engine that was also used in the 1961 Chrysler 300-G. Plymouth also offered the same engine on a limited basis. The 413 used in the 1961 Chrysler cars was the first shot fired in what would become an all-out war for horsepower supremacy in the 1960s.

Chrysler's lesser Dodge and Plymouth divisions had come alive in the mid-1950s with a combination of smart styling and solid engineering. Their dowdy exteriors were transformed into sexy shapes by designer Virgil Exner. He lowered the cars, and added fins and a forward lean that conveyed a bold, powerful vision of the future. Both divisions took a cue from the Chrysler letter cars and added their own special high-performance models. The Plymouth Fury and Dodge D-500 set the stage for the muscle cars of the 1960s. Chrysler's innovative engine design and superior engineering created the Hemi, a superior wedge engine, ram induction, torsion bar suspension, an outstanding automatic transmission, and advanced body structure. As the 1960s began, both Dodge and Plymouth were struggling to find their place in the ever changing automobile market. Both backed away from high-performance packages and bet the future on new exteriors, but Exner's designs lacked the impact they had in the 1950s. Chrysler was stumbling along a dark and dangerous path in the early 1960s. Luckily, a bright light was just around the corner.

(previous) Once the Hemi's domination of NASCAR was complete, Chrysler turned to drag racing and built a series of lightweight Dodge and Plymouth sedans to compete.

Dodge went to extreme measures to lighten its cars for drag racing. On its Hemi cars they removed the high-beam light and extended the grille to cover the opening.

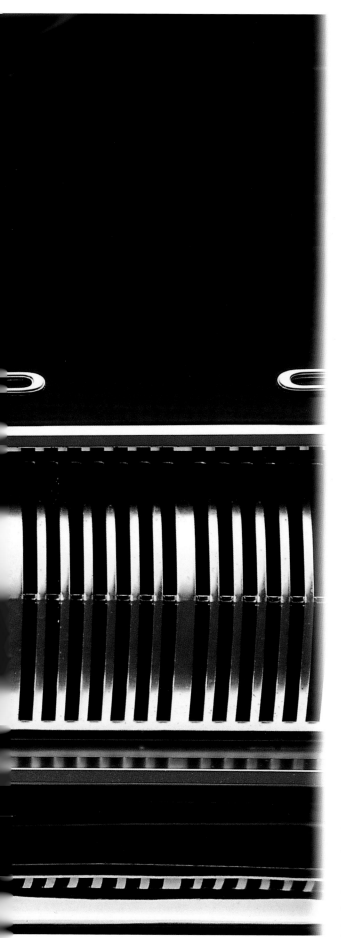

HORSEPOWER AND RACING DOMINATE THE EARLY 1960s

The automotive world changed fast in the late 1950s and early 1960s. The penchant for high-horsepower luxury cars was waning and the interest in racing was on the rise. NASCAR found that running passenger cars at exceptionally high speeds on a paved track attracted more people, media attention, and money than the typical few junkers skidding around a small dirt track. Drag racing was also becoming more popular. A local drag race was the perfect place to take the family sedan for some fun. Wally Parks, then head of the National Hot Rod Association (NHRA), was acutely aware of this. In 1959 he held the NHRA's first U.S. Nationals competition in Detroit with one purpose in mind—to attract the attention of the big three automakers.

By the late 1950s each of the three American automakers had developed a V-8 engine, some more powerful than others, but all with enough power to propel the average family sedan down the new interstate highway system at or above the legal speed limit. In some instances, these powerful new V-8s were even more fuel efficient than the previous generation of six-cylinder engines.

Motor racing had always been popular in America, and the Indy 500 had become America's premier motor sport event. Chrysler got in on the action by having its cars pace the famous race throughout the 1950s. This gave Chrysler visibility to promote its new highly styled cars and powerful Hemi engine. However, there was no direct connection

One of the most unusual features of the 1961 Dodge was its "reversed" fins.

between the race cars on the Indianapolis track and the new vehicles in dealer showrooms. NASCAR made this connection.

The cars racing in this series looked just like the cars on the dealers' lots. There were no body templates or aerodynamic wings to interfere with the distinctive look of each manufacturer's car. These early NASCAR racers ran their cars with full chrome trim, including bumpers. The only thing they removed was the outside rear view mirror and hubcaps. Drivers simply painted a number and a sponsor's name (usually a local car dealership) on the side of the car. They used some sort of strap to hold down the hood and taped over the headlights.

At that time, NASCAR made it easy for just about anyone with a little skill and a few dollars to go racing. The large network of local tracks served as training grounds for aspiring drivers. In 1959, Lee Petty won the inaugural Daytona 500 driving an Oldsmobile, then went on to win the season title. Petty also campaigned a 1959 Plymouth that season—driver contracts with manufacturers were unheard of at that time.

That same year, the NHRA moved its U.S. Nationals to the Motor City's Detroit Dragway. This move was intended to attract auto executives to this relatively new form of racing. "In 1959, we were working very hard to gain the attention of the Detroit industry," recalls Wally Parks. "At the '59 Nationals we had Tex Colbert, who was the president of Chrysler, and Ed Cole, who was the president of Chevrolet, standing there making bets on whose model would win." In 1959, the cars racing in NHRA's stock classes were factory stock passenger cars with few, if any, modifications. The technology developed to improve horsepower for larger luxury cars had filtered down to the bread-and-butter vehicles, providing the average customer with tire-smoking performance. This performance gain was not lost on the multitudes of drag racing fans, which often purchased cars based on quarter-mile times.

Dodge completely redesigned its 1961 offerings. Two D-500 engine options were available, one rated at 350 horsepower and the other rated at 375 horsepower.

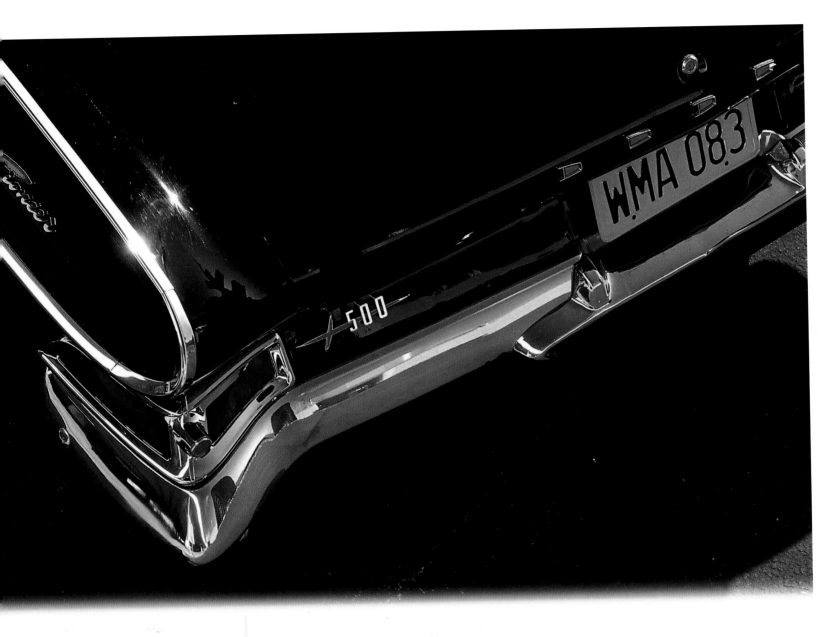

Barely visible to the right of the left taillight on this 1961 Dodge Pioneer is the "500" emblem that indicates this car is powered by one of two optional D-500 V-8s.

In 1960, when the NHRA returned to Detroit Dragway, the stock classes were filled with Detroit's latest machinery. Al Eckstrand raced a 1960 Plymouth equipped with a SonoRamic 383 engine. Eckstrand's Plymouth easily won the Super Stock Automatic (S/SA) class. The 330-horsepower engine, backed by the TorqueFlite transmission, powered Eckstrand's Plymouth to a time of 14.51 at a speed of 102.04 miles per hour. Unfortunately, Chrysler didn't take advantage of this win to capture the hearts and wallets of young men who wanted a low-cost performance car. Chevrolet, whose passenger cars won nothing of note at the 1960 Nationals, fulfilled the role of low-cost performance king.

In 1961, the new 413 ci engine was not available long enough to qualify for NHRA Super Stock competition. Chrysler's cars were being beaten on the drag strips, on the NASCAR tracks, and in the dealer showrooms. But Chrysler's cars would soon be vaulted into the hearts of every performance enthusiast because of changes that were about to take place.

One of these changes was the phenomenon of downsizing cars. This became part of Dodge and Plymouth's plan for 1962, in which both brands offered new vehicles that were smaller, lighter, and had shorter wheelbases (116 inches) than previous models. The lengths were also reduced to 202-

inches—10 inches shorter than the 1961 models. Chrysler's corporate code for these new Dodge and Plymouth platforms was "B-body."

The reduction in overall size was in response to the 1962 rollout of Chevrolet's Chevy II and Ford's Fairlane, both intermediate-size vehicles. The size of the new Dodge and Plymouth B-bodies may have been on target, but styling missed the mark. The new B-bodies had some styling cues in common with the compact Lancer/Valiant, a move that didn't sit well with consumers. The styling of both cars, the last of Exner's designs, lacked grace and continuity. The man who created the elegant Chrysler 300s of the 1950s had failed to follow mainstream automotive design.

In 1962, Dodge removed the performance-oriented D-500 from the option list, making the Polara 500 the highest level of trim available on a new Dodge. The Polara 500 featured bucket seats and a standard 305-horsepower, 361-ci engine with dual exhaust. Dodge produced the Polara 500 in three body styles: convertible, two-door hardtop, and four-door hardtop. It was embarrassing that the brand that introduced low-cost performance with the D-500 six years earlier had sunk to offer only a 305 horsepower engine as its largest engine—and to then stuff it in a four-door body with bucket seats. It appeared as though the Dodge and Plymouth performance mine was losing oxygen and all of the parakeets were dying.

But things changed suddenly in May of 1962. The 413 engine, first introduced in the 1959 Chrysler 300-E, found a new home in the engine compartments of the smaller, B-body 1962 Dodges and Plymouths. The engine wasn't a standard 413; it was a special performance version built strictly for drag racing. This engine came to be known as the Max Wedge.

81

The 1961 Dodge Dart Pioneer two-door hardtop featured a 60/40 front bench seat.

Chrysler built two iterations of the Max Wedge: a 410 horsepower version that listed for $545.00 and a 420 horsepower version that cost $612.00. The engines were identical except for compression ratio.

Dodge called its new Max Wedge engine the "Ramcharger" and Plymouth called it the "Golden Commando." Both engines were fitted with a new short ram intake with 15-inch runners, dual Carter AFB carburetors, large-port heads, and a radical, solid-lifter camshaft. As standard equipment, Chrysler installed a beefy Hurst-shifted Borg Warner three-speed manual transmission behind these engines. Chrysler made the mighty TorqueFlite an option with both engines. Up until this engine-TorqueFlite combination, automatic transmissions and racing had never mixed. Chrysler instantly changed everyone's perception.

The 1961 Dodge featured all-new styling. This Phoenix convertible was built on a 118-inch wheelbase chassis.

The new Max Wedge engine proved to be powerful and easy to tune right off the assembly line. The sturdy TorqueFlite made race car drivers out of those who had never driven a car with a manual transmission. In late 1962, young, performance-minded customers began to look at Dodge and Plymouth in a new light. The cars had a reputation on the drag strip and the low dollar-to-horsepower ratio was compelling. Only 24 (12 each) 1962 Max Wedge Plymouths and Dodges were built in 1962, and those were sent to dealers and individuals most likely to make the most of the car's performance capabilities. There was no chance to order one before the end of the 1962 model year. But in 1963, sales orders were waiting for Max Wedge Plymouths and Dodges yet to be built.

NASCAR's single four-barrel version of the Max Wedge engine didn't raise the same cloud of dust as the drag racers, but the improvement was immediate. Richard Petty, driving a Plymouth, notched his and Plymouth's first NASCAR win in 1962 at North Wilkesboro Speedway's spring race. Before the year's end, Petty would enjoy eight more wins in his Plymouth. Even though Chrysler didn't have an official NASCAR program, the NASCAR wins did give those bragging rights.

But it was the drag strip wins that herded customers. In 1962, drag racing was something almost any average car customer could accomplish. Drag strips were popping up all over the country, and finding a straight, open road and someone to race proved even easier. The powerful Max Wedge engine brought in customers who simply wanted race cars—everybody wanted to be seen with a winner, and that's what the Dodge and Plymouth salesmen counted on.

Dodge and Plymouth rode their newfound horsepower success into 1963. Thankfully,

The standard engine on all 1961 Dodge Darts, except for the convertible, was the slant six. Optional V-8 engines ranged from 318 to 413 ci.

In 1960 Dodge produced two different series of cars. The Dodge Dart with a 118-inch wheelbase and the Matador with a 122-inch wheelbase. This Phoenix convertible is one of the models in the Dart series.

The 1960 Dodge Dart Phoenix had similar styling to the larger Matador series. One of the most noticeable differences was that the tailfin ended at the taillight on the shorter Phoenix.

both cars were re-skinned for 1963 to look more mainstream. Dodge and Plymouth also tried to bring back some of the enthusiasm that the D-500 and Sport Fury had created in the 1950s. The Plymouth Sport Fury returned, as well as the Dodge Polara 500. The fanning of these sporty models' flames was in response to the overwhelming success of Chevrolet's Super Sport Impala and Ford's Galaxie 500, which offered flashy trim, bucket seats, and a wide variety of engine options. In addition to a cost lower than either the Chevy or the Ford, the Sport Fury and Polara 500 both offered a standard V-8 engine.

On the drag strip, the Max Wedge engine, now punched out to 426 ci, continued to win. Serious drag racers selected the engine with the 13:1 compression ratio rated at 425-horsepower, while street racers chose the milder 11:1 engine that produced 415. In addition to superior engines, the Dodge and Plymouth each weighed 200 pounds less than the lightest Chevy. To add insult to injury, Chrysler offered a special lightweight package for both cars: aluminum front fenders and hood. Those who never considered buying a Chrysler product discovered that they were fast and inexpensive. For customers looking for a more street-worthy engine , Plymouth offered a 383-ci, 330-horsepower Golden Commando. Dodge called this same engine the Polara V-8.

Jim Paschal and Richard Petty carried the Chrysler flag highest in NASCAR competition. Petty finished second in NASCAR points, with all of his wins on the short tracks. Ford dominated NASCAR's high-speed tracks with its new 427 engine. Since high-speed tracks were getting the most press coverage, it looked like the Fords and Mercurys were the only cars racing. Chrysler wanted the same level of success at Daytona that it enjoyed on the drag strips. This took a major engineering effort on the part of Chrysler and the development of a new engine.

Lynn Townsend, then Chrysler president, encouraged Chrysler's racing efforts in the early 1960s. He wanted performance vehicles and high-horsepower engines to be part of Chrysler's future plans. He prompted the evolution of the Max Wedge engine, and when a Chrysler product did not win at Daytona in 1963, Townsend asked, "What would it take to win the NASCAR Daytona race in February, 1964?" The reply came from Bob Hoover, head of Chrysler's race engine group. "If you want to go there and go like stink," Hoover recalls, "let's adapt the Hemi head to the race B engine." The project was approved in April 1963 and the crusade began to develop a new, race-worthy engine and have it ready in less than a year. Management's support was founded on the success of the wedge program and their desire to win at Daytona.

Engineers get excited about this kind of project, with clean sheets of paper on which to sketch and lots of money to spend on development. The only enemy was the calendar. "The early Hemis were a guiding light as to where we wanted to go," says Hoover. He knew that the Hemi was the engine that could develop the kind of power needed to win the Daytona 500. Chrysler's engine team used the fundamental engineering axiom: that more horsepower could be produced by intensive development of an existing design, rather than starting over with a completely new design. This is why they chose the existing "RB" block as a starting point and refine it, using knowledge gained from the early Hemi. The RB block is a raised-deck derivative of the B block first introduced in 1958. The raised deck allows for a longer stroke. The first RB engine appeared in 1959.

In April 1963, Hoover assigned Frank Bilk to create the layout of the head and the valve gear. Hoover had complete confidence in Bilk's design ability. "He had a great gift of visualization—something every great designer must have." Bilk tipped the entire head inboard a few degrees to allow the exhaust push rods to clear the head gasket bead. This also enhanced the flow to the intake valve. "I've been called the father of the Hemi," says Hoover. "But Frank was the real father of the Hemi. I just provided some ideas."

The placement of the exhaust valve in the Hemi's cylinder head required an extremely long and heavy rocker arm. The Hemi engine's design team decided to make the exhaust rocker arm the same length as the one on the 392 Hemi engine. This decision was based on the fact that at that

While the Hemi version gets the lion's share of the attention, the Max Wedge version of the 330 was no slouch.

time, Top Fuel dragsters running 392 ci Hemi engines were consistently turning engine speeds as high as 7,000 rpm. They knew that radical changes to that key component would jeopardize the engine's ability to reach high rpms.

Early dynamometer testing revealed a weakness in the right hand cylinder walls that eventually led to cracks. With the deadline for the Daytona race approaching, Chrysler had to ship competitors some engines that they knew would not last a full race, but that could be installed for inspection and run in qualifications. While the drama was unfolding at the track, redesigned blocks that would be more durable were being cast and machined in Detroit. These engines were delivered just days before the race.

Richard Petty, a lanky, second-generation racer from the south whose father had driven Plymouths, was the winner of the 1964 Daytona 500. Chrysler's new Hemi engine became the king of NASCAR's hill and sent Ford's design team into overdrive trying to create an engine to compete with it.

The instant success of the NASCAR single four-barrel-carbureted version of the Hemi was overshadowed by the fact that, in testing, the dual-quad drag racing version wasn't any quicker than the 426 Max Wedge engine. The release of the Hemi drag race cars was delayed until June while engineers worked on the problem. They found that a new camshaft was needed. Once released, the new Hemi cars ended up racing each other for class honors, because in 1964, there were no cars to match the Hemi's performance.

There were no external Hemi emblems on a 1964 Dodge. While not designed for the street, a few owners did take them for short cruises.

Chrysler built two production-line versions of the Hemi in 1964: a 415-horsepower version that featured an 11:1 compression, and the 425-horsepower version that had 12.5:1. Both used the cross-ram intake with dual, four-barrel carburetors. The first 1964 Hemi cars raced in NASCAR competition were not built on the assembly line. Instead, Hemi engines and heavy-duty components were put in production cars at the various race shops. Chrysler also made an over-the-counter kit to convert Hemi-equipped 1964 Plymouth Belvederes or Dodge 440 hardtops into NASCAR racers. This kit included a single four-barrel intake manifold, headers, and a host of heavy-duty components. Chrysler created this kit to encourage more individuals to race Dodges and Plymouths in NASCAR.

In 1964, Dodge and Plymouth didn't forget those who wanted high-performance street racers. Dodge offered the Polara with bucket seats and a 330-horsepower, 383-ci engine. Plymouth offered the Sport Fury with the 330-horsepower 383. Plymouth one-upped Dodge with the introduction of the optional 426-S engine. Plymouth took the basic 426 RB Max Wedge race engine and detuned it for the

When the 1964 race Hemis were released, they were equipped with a dual quad cross ram intake manifold similar to the ones used on the Max Wedge engines. Both Holley (shown) and Carter carburetors were used.

street. They added a single, four-barrel carburetor, smaller heads, and a mild hydraulic-lifter cam to obtain 365 horsepower and 475 ft-lb of torque. Plymouth added a standard Hurst-shifted four-speed transmission and offered the TorqueFlite automatic as an option. Plymouth priced the 426-S engine option at a stiff $482.95. For that price the buyer also received a heavy-duty suspension and brake package. When *Motor Trend* magazine tested a Sport Fury with the 426-S engine in January 1964, it clicked off a quarter mile in 15.2 seconds at 95 miles per hour. Its skinny, 7.50x14 tires and 2.73 gears (no Sure Grip differential here) hindered the car's performance.

In 1964, the Pontiac GTO and the Ford Mustang were the two hottest cars on the road. Pontiac built the GTO by placing a hefty 389-ci engine into an intermediate-sized body. A comparison of the 1964 GTO and the 1964 Plymouth Sport Fury showed that the Plymouth's 116-inch wheelbase measured only one inch longer than the GTO's, and that the Plymouth's overall length exceeded the GTO's by only two inches. The Fury's 426-S engine produced 365 horsepower, compared to the GTO's optional engine at 348 horsepower. The Plymouth weighed 200 pounds less and cost about the same as a comparably optioned GTO. With equal gearing, the Plymouth should have blown the doors off any GTO, but the GTO had image—and lots of it. Even though a Plymouth had won the Daytona 500 and was one of the fastest cars on the drag strip, it still carried its "taxicab" baggage of the past. To many young enthusiasts, its flashy chrome side moldings and whitewall tires still said, "Grandpa's car." Plymouth could have cashed in on the emerging muscle car market, but instead directed its high-performance efforts toward the new Barracuda in order to compete with the Mustang. It would be a few years before the Chrysler B-body was recognized as a true muscle car in the same class as the GTO.

Chrysler restructured its Dodge and Plymouth car lines in 1965 by creating new full-sized vehicles (C-bodies) and relegating the B-bodies to traditional transportation cars with only a hint of high-performance. Previously, Dodge and Plymouth B-bodies fit Chrysler's mold as full-size cars, but now they were marketed as intermediates with the introduction of the new, larger, C-body chassis. Dodge reclaimed the Coronet name abandoned at the end of the 1959 model year, and added it to the 117-inch-wheelbase B-body. The styling of the new Dodge could be described as almost "boxy." Plymouth narrowed its 1965 B-bodies to a Belvedere series built on a 116-inch wheelbase. Like the 1965 Dodge Coronets, the new Plymouth Belvedere was nicely styled, but not earthshaking. Dodge called its 1965, top-of-the-line B-body the Coronet 500, and Plymouth positioned the Belvedere Satellite as its top model. Both were offered in a two-door hardtop or convertible, featuring standard bucket seats and a small V-8, with the 426-S engine optional. The new B-bodies were poised to do battle with GM's successful Chevelle, LeMans, and Cutlass series of cars—but unfortunately, didn't have the weapons to do so.

Chrysler's 1965 introduction of the new C-body Dodge Polara and Plymouth Fury indicated that they wanted to battle Ford and General Motors head to head. Plymouth tried to position its new C-body Sport Fury in the same class as the Chevrolet Impala SS. But, Chevrolet's smoothly rounded 1965 models instantly made the angular Sport Fury look dated. Dodge positioned its special 1965 Monaco C-body to compete with Pontiac's sporty Grand Prix. It too lost against Pontiac's sexy new curves. However, Plymouth scored a coup when officials chose a Sport Fury convertible to pace the 1965 Indianapolis 500.

Chrysler's 1965 racing plans were severely affected by rule changes. In order to race in the 1965 NASCAR series, a manufacturer had to build 500 cars with the designated race engine and then

Dodge's 1964 Hemi-powered drag racing sedans were stripped of the original rear bench seats, and two lightweight bucket seats replaced the front seat.

The Dodge 330 was the least expensive of the three Dodge models in 1964. Along with being the favorite of librarians and grandparents, drag racers loved this body style because it was the lightest of all the Dodge models.

DETAIL

STAGE 3

Unlike the Hemi-powered drag-racing model, the street-going Max Wedge 330 featured a high-beam headlight.

The 1964 Dodge 330 interior featured a simple bench seat. The up-scale Polara 500 offered bucket seats.

The development of Chrysler's
TorqueFlite automatic transmission is
one of the key factors in the success
of its drag-racing program.
Pushbutton controls were last seen
on the 1964 models.

make those cars available to the general public. The Hemi's utter domination of the NASCAR tracks in 1964 led to this ban. Ford was also ready to release a single overhead cam, 427-ci engine for the 1965 season. NASCAR's new rule changed both Chrysler and Ford's plans and put a halt to an impending manufacturer's war of building one-off race engines. Chrysler withdrew support of its NASCAR teams and focused on forms of drag racing where the Hemi was legal. Ford also focused on drag racing in 1965, where its new single overhead cam 427 could be legally raced. In an act of defiance to the new rules, Richard Petty, NASCAR's biggest name in 1964, walked away from the oval tracks and drag raced a Hemi-powered Barracuda Funny Car in 1965. There were, however, a few diehard Chrysler competitors who raced the larger 121-inch wheelbase C-body Dodge Polara and Plymouth Fury in NASCAR.

Chrysler's success in drag racing prompted them to build cars that would be legal in NHRA's Super Stock class for 1965. The cars they built were similar to the Dodge and Plymouth Hemi-powered cars released the previous year. Chrysler started with its lightest B-body vehicles: a Belvedere I two-door sedan and a Coronet two-door sedan. With some elegant engineering, Chrysler reduced the weight of both vehicles and added the most sophisticated Hemi engine to date. Plymouth coded the 101 cars it

By 1964 tailfins were just a bad memory.

built as R01; and Dodge coded the 101 cars it built as W01. But these cars are best known as A-990—Chrysler's internal engineering code. These cars were sold through regular dealer channels with certain high-profile racers having first choice. The Plymouth listed for $4,671 and the Dodge for $4,717.

These new A-990s were the last and most sophisticated race cars to be built on a factory assembly line (both the Dodge and Plymouth were built at Chrysler's Lynch Road assembly plant). All future cars of this type would be assembled at an offsite location. All the A-990 cars were built at the end of 1964 and in early 1965. Nearly all were built as dealer sales bank vehicles. Produced as race cars, they were delivered to the customers without any warranty.

Dodge and Plymouth A-990 cars were based on the lightest B-body two-door sedan. Chrysler selected this body because it was 40 pounds lighter than a two-door hardtop. Lightweight doors, front fenders, and hood were added to further reduce the vehicle's weight. The cars lacked the sound deadener and body sealers normally applied to a standard passenger car. Chrysler dropped all the exterior bright trim usually applied to these sedans. The glass, except for the windshield, was constructed from Corning .080-inch tempered glass. These cars were further lightened by the omission of the radio, heater, armrests, sun visors, and right-hand windshield wiper. To reduce weight even more, Dodge removed the inner headlight on its

Included with the 426 Max Wedge engine in 1964 were a set of 3-inch-diameter factory exhaust cutouts. This allowed the customer to go directly from the showroom to the drag strip.

(opposite) Dodge produced two 426-ci Ramcharger V-8s for 1964: one rated at 415 horsepower and the other rated at 425 horsepower. Both of these Max Wedge engines used the cross ram intake and dual Carter AFB carburetors.

The 1963 Plymouth Sport Fury was offered in two-door hardtop and convertible body styles. It was Plymouth's premium model that year featuring standard bucket seats with a center console.

The 1963 Plymouth Sport Fury's side moldings were fitted with a machined-turned anodized aluminum insert.

A-990 cars. Chrysler bolted two lightweight bucket seats to the front floor and skipped the rear seat. A standard passenger car carpet covered the floor, but to save weight, Chrysler dropped the padding. The cars were trimmed in a Medium Tan metallic vinyl with no options for the interior style or color.

One basic maxim in drag racing is to put as much weight on the rear wheels as possible. Chrysler used a little suspension trickery to redistribute the A-990s weight to the rear. The wheelbase on a production 1965 Coronet measured 117-inches, and on a Belvedere, 116-inches. Chrysler reduced the wheelbase on all of the A-990 race cars to 115-inches by pulling the rear wheels forward, using special rear spring hangers. This effectively placed more weight on the rear wheels. This increased traction at the start of the race, where it counts the most.

Chrysler put its dual-quad race Hemi under the A-990's hood. Engineers rated this engine at 425 horsepower, the same as the previous year, but it featured several components that saved weight and increased performance. The most noticeable improvement was the use of aluminum cylinder heads. This would be the only 426 Hemi engine to use these heads. For 1965, Chrysler selected magnesium, instead of aluminum, as the material for the dual-quad intake manifold. To further lighten the cars, Chrysler added an aluminum water pump. Only two transmissions were offered: a Hurst-shifted four-speed manual that included a steel clutch housing (designed to contain a clutch explosion) and a TorqueFlite automatic. Most A-990 cars were fitted with the TorqueFlite.

The A-990s dominated drag racing's Super Stock class throughout 1965, and many still race today. Ford installed several of its 427 single-overhead-cam engines in specially-prepared 1965 Mustangs that ran in the Factory Experimental class. Chrysler countered by building twelve altered-wheelbase Dodges and Plymouths and with that, the Funny Car was born.

Many things would change in 1966 due to the emerging muscle car market and Chrysler's desire to return to NASCAR racing. The Hemi would return in a new form and promote the lowly Chrysler B-body car to legendary status, and the name of a silly cartoon character would be affixed to one of the greatest muscle cars of all time.

Tucked neatly under the floor pan of the Max Wedge–equipped 1963 Plymouths were a set of factory installed exhaust cutouts.

(previous) *The 1970 Road Runner was available in three body styles: hardtop (shown), coupe, or convertible. When optioned with the Hemi engine, 15-inch wheels were standard with F-60x15 raised white letter tires.*

HEMI

The functional Ramcharger hood scoops were standard on Hemi-equipped 1969 Dodge Coronet R/Ts.

CHRYSLER'S B-BODY MUSCLE CARS 1966–1971

Lynn Townsend understood business as well as he understood cars. At six-feet, two-inches tall, he cut a wide swath while roaming the styling studios at Chrysler or visiting small Chrysler suppliers. He wasn't afraid to make cuts where necessary in the interest of the company. He closed some plants, consolidated others, and even sold the company's fleet of private airplanes. He restructured the company's dealer organization and distribution network. His business sense and vision propelled him to the cover of *Time* magazine under the banner "The comeback story of U.S. business."

Townsend set out to make Chrysler dealers more visible on Main Street America. After a lengthy trip around the nation visiting Chrysler dealers, he returned to Detroit convinced there were more "orange-roofed" Howard Johnson's restaurants than Chrysler dealers. He commissioned the New York PR firm of Lippincott & Margulies to create a highly identifiable symbol for Chrysler, resulting in the Pentastar: a thin, white star on a bright blue, pentagon-shaped background. By the beginning of 1966, more than 5,000 of these blue and white signs had been installed at Chrysler dealerships. The Pentastar showed up on almost everything connected to Chrysler, even the small lapel pins worn by Chrysler executives. Chrysler's engineers at Cape Canaveral wore them on their hard hats, and they were featured on every piece of documentation Chrysler produced. Soon the Chrysler Pentastar logo became a symbol people could easily recognize and trust.

Thanks to Townsend, the mid-1960s was also a time when Chrysler Financial began to play a larger role in Chrysler's profits and future. Townsend recruited accountant Gordon Areen to head the organization. Up until then, financing of Chrysler cars primarily depended on banks and independent finance companies—both of which could be fickle. Ford and GM had their own finance arms and were relatively free of the ups and downs of the finance world. Chrysler Financial ensured the rates and down payment schedules given to new car customers were competitive and fair. This helped dealers sell cars and helped Chrysler's bottom line.

Townsend was also committed to continuing Chrysler racing programs, especially NASCAR. In order to do so with the Hemi engine, they had to produce a street version. But Chrysler didn't place

the Hemi into a production car to dominate the muscle car world—it just so happened that by installing the Hemi engine in a passenger car, Chrysler inadvertently created a legend. With the release of the street Hemi in 1966, Chrysler instantly moved to the head table at the horsepower banquet.

Unfortunately, Chrysler's 1966 B-body offerings looked as though they were milled out of a solid block of steel. The new B-bodies had sharp edges, while General Motor's entire line of cars featured smoothly rounded edges. Even Ford's offerings for 1966 were years ahead of Chrysler's. Chrysler missed the styling train in 1962, and by 1966 still hadn't found the ticket booth. The 1966 Dodge and Plymouth B-body cars would have looked stylish in 1963, but for the 1966 model year, they were much too stodgy.

The 1966 Belvedere and Coronet models suffered further from a lack of performance options. The pedestrian 318- and 361-ci engines were adequate for trips to the supermarket, but not considered performance engines. The 325-horsepower 383 would have been an acceptable performance engine in 1963, but in 1966, the more powerful muscle car engines offered by the competition clearly overshadowed it. The gap in cost and horsepower between the 383 and the Hemi was huge. This problem would be solved in 1967 with the introduction of the 440-ci engine, but for 1966, the Hemi was the only game in town.

Chrysler did not introduce the street Hemi engine with the intention to rule the highways; rather, they wanted to make the powerful engine legal for NASCAR racing. Chrysler engineers didn't re-engineer the Hemi for street use, merely detuned it. The basic street Hemi engine retained all the strength and durability features of the original race Hemi engine. Chrysler reduced the compression ratio to run on premium pump gas and gave the engine a less-aggressive cam profile. Instead of a large cross-ram intake manifold, Chrysler added a new aluminum manifold that

In 1967, Plymouth introduced its Belvedere-based GTX. In addition to a standard 375-horsepower 440-ci engine, Plymouth included chrome road wheels, red line tires, hood scoops, and bucket seats.

The 1967 Plymouth GTX featured a pit stop–style gas cap on the left quarter panel.

mounted two Carter AFB carburetors. Chrysler topped off the engine with a large, chrome-plated, low-restriction air cleaner.

Chrysler took the race proven RB-style block they first installed in its race cars and made minor modifications to create the street Hemi block. The connecting rods and forged crankshaft were identical to those in the race engines. So were the rocker arms, pushrods, and valves. Chrysler installed a mild, 276-degree solid-lifter camshaft. For camshaft durability, the rates on the valve springs were lowered.

The Hemi's exceptional breathing capability remained intact in the new street version, thanks to the new dual quad intake manifold. This intake mounted two Carter AFB carbure-tors with a combined flow rate of approximately 1,100 cfm. Chrysler included progressive linkage that allowed most driving to use the rear carburetor, with the front carburetor poised to open based on the amount of adrenaline activating the driver's right foot. The uncompli-cated but effective Carter AFB carburetors included a secondary air valve that tailored the airflow to match engine demand. The rear carburetor included an automatic choke and received exhaust heat. These simple features enhanced drivability on the street without sacri-ficing performance.

The 1964 and 1965 race Hemis were fitted with tubular exhaust headers. Chrysler knew these weren't practical for street driving and created an elegant pair of cast-iron exhaust manifolds for the street Hemi. The right side manifold swept back smartly and housed a valve that directed warm exhaust gases to the base of the rear carburetor. Chrysler designed the left side manifold to clear the

steering box. Because of this, it was less streamlined than its mate on the other side of the engine. Both manifolds connected to exhaust pipes measuring 2 1/2 inches in diameter.

The street Hemi was a magnificent engine, but Chrysler didn't just give them away. The cost of the street Hemi option in 1966 drove up the price of a standard Plymouth Satellite to that of a new Corvette equipped with a small block engine. Buying a car in this rarefied air posed a unique problem for the buyer. Should he spend an extra $1,110 for the Hemi or buy a Corvette? Chrysler's marketing and sales groups forecasted sales of the Hemi option in the 5,000-7,000-unit range. Actual sales figures for the Hemi option in 1966 were slightly more than 2,700. While disappointing, the image of the Hemi engine, and the NASCAR racers who won races with them, drew attention to both Dodge and Plymouth and brought customers into the show-rooms. Today, this phenomenon is called the "halo effect." Back in 1966 it was called, "win on Sunday; sell on Monday."

The Hemi engine and its associated package of heavy-duty, four-speed transmission or TorqueFlite automatic and beefed-up drive-line was well-engineered and bulletproof, but customers got little else to show for their money. A small Hemi badge graced the front fender and Goodyear Blue Streak tires were added. There was no muscle car panache of a GTO or SS396

In 1967, Dodge and Plymouth each built 55 special Hemi-equipped B-body cars designed to dominate NHRA's SS/B class. This Dodge, code WO23, came from the factory with a large hood scoop.

Following the muscle car trend of the mid-1960s of adding a series of two or three consonants to create a name, Plymouth named its 1967 Belvedere performance model "GTX."

Chevelle, which sported hood scoops, chrome tailpipe extensions, and sporty wheels fitted with red-line tires. The popular GTO offered its famous tri-power carburetion with chrome engine accents. The SS396 Chevelle could be ordered with a bench seat and three different engines ranging from 325 to 375 horsepower. However, these cars did have a two-year jump on Chrysler.

The 1966 Dodge Charger

Dodge introduced its stylish new 1966 Charger in a halftime television commercial during the 1966 Rose Bowl game. The ad's tag line of, "Plant one of these in your driveway," caught the attention of the viewers as they got their first glimpse of Dodge's sleek new production Charger. The Charger's extreme fastback roofline, curved side glass, and hidden headlights were in step with the latest automotive styling trends. The new Charger would be in Dodge showrooms by spring.

The 1966 Dodge Charger evolved from two concept cars that Chrysler had built and displayed in the mid-1960s. The first Charger was shown throughout the 1964 car show season. Dodge started with a Polara convertible and transformed it into a race-inspired, two-seat roadster. A low, wraparound windscreen replaced the traditional windshield. The rear seats were covered with a panel that extended from the front edge of the deck lid to the rear of the twin bucket seats. A wide roll bar featured a pair of futuristic headrests. The hood scoop, magnesium wheels, and quarter-panel exhaust ports alluded to Dodge's racing heritage. Then in 1965, Dodge overwhelmed the public with its Charger II. The show attendees had no idea how close this car would be to what they would see in the showroom the following year. The fastback roof and sculpted sides were precursors of the production version.

Chrysler allowed Dodge to build this upscale, personal sports sedan to complement its line of cars without competing directly with the cars Plymouth was marketing. Plymouth held down the lower end of the market and had been selling its sporty Barracuda since 1964. Chrysler positioned Dodge at the higher end market and did not have a pony car like the Barracuda in its lineup. Another reason Dodge added the Charger was to counter the new sport sedans. Buick introduced its sporty Riviera in 1963, which was updated in 1966 by Vice President of Design Bill Mitchell. Oldsmobile joined the group in 1966 with its new front-wheel-drive Toronado. Ford's Thunderbird was the veteran of the group and had owned the sports sedan market since 1958. All of these cars were either built with, or offered, a high-performance engine option. Seeing a new market niche was reason enough for Dodge to create the Charger.

Dodge lacked the funds to create an all-new platform for a relatively small, but highly visible, market segment. To save money, the 1966 Dodge Charger was a "make-from" car. Dodge took its B-body Coronet and added new quarter panels and a fastback roof to create the Charger. Even though the Charger had its roots in the Coronet, Dodge's design team did a wonderful job of creating a striking car without breaking the bank.

Jimmy Addison owned Woodward Avenue in the late 1960s with this Hemi-powered 1967 Plymouth GTX, the Silver Bullet.

The 1966 Charger quarter panels boasted the same sculpted outline as the B-body Coronet. Dodge designers raised the Charger's rear wheel openings, thereby giving the car a decidedly sporty appearance. The full-width grille consisted of chrome-plated, slender, bars. These bars continued across the headlight doors that, when closed, created an uninterrupted expanse of grille. This design theme also graced the tail, where a single, six-lamp taillight extended across the rear of the car.

Dodge fitted the new Charger with four vinyl-covered bucket seats separated by a full-length console. The individual rear bucket seats were hinged and could fold forward

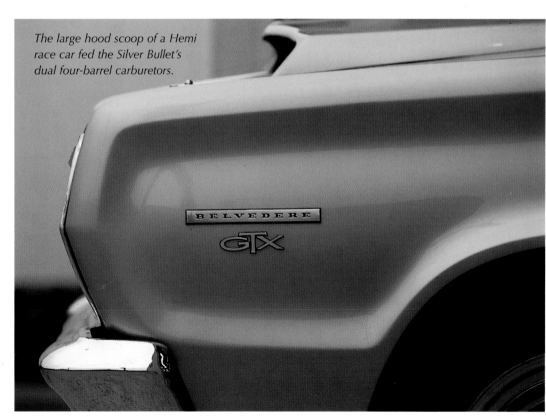

The large hood scoop of a Hemi race car fed the Silver Bullet's dual four-barrel carburetors.

BELVEDERE

GTX

In the image on the car:

AL ECKSTRAND

Charger

AMERICAN COMMANDO DRAG TEAM
SANTA POD RACEWAY, BEDFORDSHIRE, ENGLAND

Performance by
Mark Wilson
Gainesville, Fl

With Thanks
to
Latimer Motors Uk.
Tel: 01144 1323 641525

LAWMAN

DODGE
425 hp
HEMI

DANGER
HIGH VOLTAGE
KEEP OUT
AUTHORIZED
PERSONNEL ONLY

In 1966, Al Eckstrand, then a Chrysler corporate lawyer, toured U.S. Military bases in Europe giving safe-driving demonstrations with this Hemi-powered 1966 Charger.

creating cargo space more typically found in a station wagon. Dodge's clever designers redesigned the B-body instrument panel, housing the gauges in four large circular pods. A 150-mile-per-hour speedometer and a 6,000-rpm tachometer were standard equipment.

Dodge gave the 1966 Charger a standard 318-ci V-8 rated at 230 horsepower. Optional engines included the 361-ci, 265-horsepower V-8, the 383-ci, 325-horsepower V-8, and the 425-horsepower Hemi. When a 383 or Hemi were selected, Dodge added a small badge to the front fender. Dodge limited the transmission selection on these optional V-8s to a TorqueFlite automatic or four-speed manual, both with a console-mounted shifter.

The 1966 Dodge Charger had many of the same attributes that made the early Chrysler letter cars so successful. Chrysler's letter car design philosophy of "less is more" rang true again with the Charger. Chrome trim was used specifically to highlight the car's character lines. Interior colors were limited, but the customer could select from 17 exterior colors. No two-tone paint schemes were available. The new Charger's base 318-ci engine lacked the brutish knockout punch of the standard Hemi engine in the early letter cars, but a buyer could still get the new 426 Hemi as an option. The base 1966 Charger listed for $3,122, more than $1,000 less than a

Buick Riviera or Oldsmobile Toronado. The addition of the optional Hemi engine ate up that difference and placed the new Charger in a class of its own.

What Chrysler's 1966 B-bodies lacked in appearance, they made up for in raw Hemi horsepower and a sophisticated drive train. Without the Hemi (and Dodge Charger), Chrysler's 1966 offerings might have been forgotten, lost among mainstream cars of the year. Chrysler's astute move of converting a race engine for the street is what made these cars special.

In 1967, Chrysler woke up to the fact that they needed to offer the performance buyer more than one exceptionally big engine and a set of Blue Streak tires. Chrysler also realized that names such as Satellite and Coronet didn't resonate with young muscle car buyers—their parents and grandparents drove those. Their peers, however, were driving GTOs, 442s, SS396s, and GT-350s. These were imposing cars with impressive names that had as much visual appeal as they did horsepower.

Both of Chrysler's B-body offerings received mild facelifts for 1967. These minimal changes to the Coronet and Belvedere models were not enough to disguise the 1966 body underneath. What did set them apart,

The 1966 Dodge Charger's interior featured four individual bucket seats separated by a full-length console. The rear seat backs were able to fold down, creating a large luggage compartment with a flat floor.

117

By the late 1960s, Chrysler's mighty 426 Hemi was firmly and permanently enthroned at the top of the performance heap.

The 1966 and 1967 Dodge Chargers featured a full-width grille composed of slender chrome bars. Dodge artfully camouflaged the hidden headlight doors to match the grille.

however, were the new performance-based R/T and GTX packages. To its Coronet, Dodge added the name R/T, which stood for Road and Track. Plymouth's GTX had no distinct meaning, but the string of consonants sounded powerful and sexy. A new 440-ci engine was introduced to fill the performance gap between the 383 and the Hemi. This promised to be a good year for Mopar fans that warmed to promotions for the new Dodge "Rebellion" and to Plymouth's efforts to "Win you over."

The new R/T and GTX models could be purchased as either two-door hardtops or convertibles. Both were similarly equipped with standard bucket seats, center consoles, heavy-duty suspensions, chrome wheels, and red line tires. The R/T featured unique hood louvers and the GTX boasted twin hoods scoops. Sport stripes were also available on the GTX. The less-is-more theory of exterior ornamentation was applied to both of these cars, with only tasteful rocker moldings and thin wheel opening moldings on the sides. Dodge placed red-inlayed R/T emblems on the quarter panels, deck lids, and grilles. Plymouth added small GTX emblems to the front fenders and on the deck lids. Although these exterior treatments were understated, they communicated to the world that these cars weren't standard grocery-getters.

Chrysler moved in the right direction by making the standard engine in the 1967 Dodge R/T

The 1968 Road Runner was inexpensive and, with the standard 383 engine, could beat almost any other muscle car on the street. With the Hemi it was unbeatable.

In 1969, Plymouth and Dodge release the 390-horsepower Six Pack engine in specially equipped Road Runners and Super Bees. The package included a lift-off fiberglass hood and big red line tires. Hubcaps, an annoying extra when racing, were not part of the option.

and Plymouth GTX the 440-cubic inch, 375-horsepower RB engine. A 350-horsepower version of the 440-ci engine first appeared in 1966 in Chrysler's Newport, 300, and New Yorker. Chrysler installed it in these heavy vehicles because of the massive 480 ft-lb of torque it produced at a low 2,800rpm. When they installed it in the R/T and GTX, they added free-flowing heads with bigger valves and a long-duration, hydraulic-lifter camshaft. With these changes, the 440 now produced 375 horsepower at 4,600rpm and 480 ft-lb of torque at 3,200rpm. The torque figure for the 440 is the most interesting because the Hemi only produced 490 ft-lb at 4,000rpm. Dodge named this engine the "Magnum" and Plymouth called it the "Super Commando"—gutsy names for a gutsy engine.

The Hemi was the only optional engine for the R/T and GTX. However, Dodge and Plymouth buyers could order the Hemi in any of the Coronet and Belvedere models. The most interesting Hemi-powered, B-bodies built in 1967 were those built for NHRA's Super Stock B class. This special, one-year-only option was listed as WO23 for the Dodge and RO23 for the Plymouth. Only 55 Dodge Coronet 440s and 55 Plymouth Belvedere IIs featured this option (NHRA required 50 cars per make). The packages were identical, which consisted of the least expensive white two-door hardtop with a black bench-seat interior. To lower weight, Chrysler omitted all body sound-deadening materials, radios, and heaters. Engineers placed the battery on the right side of the luggage

The 440 Six Pack engine featured three large Holley two-barrel carburetors mounted on an Edelbrock aluminum intake manifold.

(main) *The Dodge Charger set a benchmark for automotive styling in the 1960s. This particular 1969 Charger R/T (Road and Track) was optioned with a luggage rack and bumblebee stripe-delete.*

(top right) *Dodge designers placed a racing-style gas cap on top of the 1969 Charger's left quarter panel.*

(bottom right) *Dodge Chargers came with a wide variety of V-8 engines, but only the Chargers optioned with a Hemi received any external engine identification.*

Dodge's second-generation Charger featured a Coke-bottle shape with gentle flaring of the quarter panels and front fenders. This 1969 R/T has a white bumblebee stripe. The taillights for 1969 were rectangular.

In 1969, Dodge offered two special packages for its Charger: The R/T offered standard 440 performance and the SE offered a high level of trim with leather seats. It's exceptionally unusual to see both on one Charger, especially with a factory sun roof.

compartment to aid traction and weight distribution. A large hood scoop, similar to the one installed on the A-990 race cars, was the only distinguishing feature between the standard hardtop and the W023 and R023 cars.

Chrysler installed the 425-horsepower Hemi engine in all of the W023 and RO23 cars. This was a regular production Hemi engine, not a hand-built race engine. Four-speed manual-shift models were fitted with a special NHRA-approved, explosion-proof bellhousing and a 4.88 Dana Sure Grip rear axle. The cars optioned with TorqueFlite transmissions were fitted with special 2,300-2,500rpm stall-speed torque converters and 8 3/4 Sure Grip rear axles with 4.86 gears. To win races, the owner simply added a set of headers and slicks.

Dodge did well with its new Charger in 1966. Unfortunately, the public quickly tired of the extreme fastback, and Charger sales took a 60-percent dive in 1967. Dodge made a few changes to the 1967 model to correct what were perceived as deficiencies. To allow a fifth passenger, Dodge modified the center console to add a temporary seat between the two front buckets. Dodge also

In 1969, the Dodge R/T logo had become as well known as GT, SS, or GTO. For those buying a Dodge Charger R/T, it meant a minimum of 375 horsepower and a host of standard heavy-duty components.

Eight-track tapes were state-of-the-art entertainment in 1969. For an additional $196.26, the buyer of a new 1969 Dodge Charger could add an optional AM radio with tape player so he could listen to his Credence tapes.

added chrome wheels and Red Line tires to the option list. In addition to the 325-horsepower 383 and the Hemi, the hot 440-ci, 375-horsepower engine could be ordered.

Now that Chrysler understood image and engines, it had to bring its styling up to date. That would happen in 1968.

If Chrysler had introduced its 1968 B-body offerings (and Charger) in 1967, they would have swept away the entire country. Unfortunately, 1968 was one hell of a year for new car introductions. Chrysler's beautiful new cars became part of the show, but not all of it. General Motors took center stage with the introduction of its Mako-Shark–styled Corvette. For 1968, the beautifully restyled Pontiac GTO offered an Endura front bumper, hidden headlights, and standard 400-ci engine. The editors at *Motor Trend* magazine were so impressed with the new GTO that they named it "Car of the Year" for 1968. Chevrolet also redesigned and upgraded its lowly Nova to mid-size status and offered big block engines with horsepower ratings as high as 375. Ford's designers sharpened their mid-size design pencils and created the Torino.

Chrysler's 1968 B-body cars were almost as historically significant as the Flight Sweep designs of 1957. They featured smoothly rounded curves that were a vast departure from Chrysler's angular 1967 models. These new B-bodies looked as good as their General Motors and Ford counterparts. For 1968, the Coronet name returned and anchored the Dodge B-body line, and the Belvedere was

Plymouth's base B-body. Dodge also redesigned its 1968 B-bodied Charger into one of the most beautiful cars of the decade.

Plymouth's product planners and marketing staff had the job of creating a muscle car from the fashionably restyled 1968 Belvedere. The upscale GTX returned in 1968 and a new name appeared that rocked the muscle car world—Road Runner. Plymouth designed the Road Runner as an inexpensive thrill ride for the street. Both the Road Runner and GTX shared many of the same features, including a blacked-out grille and distinctive hood with non-functional, side-facing vents. Appliqués were added to the sides of these vents denoting the engine displacement or, in the case of the Hemi, "HEMI" was spelled out. Chrome wheels were again available along with red line tires for both the GTX and Road Runner.

Dodge's product planners were not asleep at the muscle car switch. They crafted their own version of the Road Runner: the Super Bee. They based it on a stripped-down version

Dodge designers added a center divider on the grille of the 1969 Dodge Charger. F70x14 red line tires were standard with the R/T.

This 1969 Dodge Coronet R/T was Dodge's counterpart to the Plymouth GTX. Like the GTX, it featured a standard 375-horsepower 440-ci engine. This car has the optional Hemi engine.

Non-functional quarter panel scoops were standard on all 1969 Dodge Coronet R/Ts.

Chrome GTX emblems were attached to the quarter panels of the 1968 Plymouth GTX. The twin rocker-panel stripes could be deleted.

The success of the 1967 Plymouth GTX encouraged Plymouth to continue the series in 1968. The 1968 GTX proved to be Plymouth's upscale muscle car while the new Road Runner was the blue-collar street fighter.

The 1969 Plymouth GTX had a lengthy list of standard features including bucket seats and a 375-horsepower engine; the only optional engine was the Hemi. Instead of body side stripes, Plymouth blacked out the lower portion of the body on all 1969 GTXs.

of the Coronet R/T. It shared a distinctive power-bulge hood with the R/T and featured bumblebee stripes.

The key to Chrysler's 1968 B-bodies was horsepower. Chrysler installed a 335-horsepower 383 as the base engine for the Road Runner and Super Bee. Chrysler brought this engine to life by fitting it with the same heads and cam as the 440. This superb engine was backed by either a four-speed or TorqueFlite automatic. Chrysler continued to offer the healthy 440-cubic inch, 375-horsepower V-8 as standard equipment in the Plymouth GTX and Dodge R/T. The Hemi was optional in all of these cars.

The concept of the Road Runner—a freshly restyled car, stripped of frills, with a powerful engine that will run the quarter-mile at a speed of 100 miles per hour, and a sticker price of $3,000—was brilliant. Chrysler's target market for the Road Runner was young men who had grown up in the early and mid-1960s reading about high performance cars and drag racing. This group wanted an inexpensive muscle car with plenty of image to cruise the local burger stands. The speed of 100 miles per hour in the quarter mile had become a benchmark for performance and the target of the Road Runner's product planners. They knew that a car similar to Pontiac's original GTO—a big engine, stripped of frills, and reasonably priced (under $3,000)—would capture the muscle car market. Plymouth planners settled on a two-door coupe body style because it was the least expensive and lightest. It was fitted with a simple bench seat and rubber floor mats. Frill removal went as far as removing the rear seat, but that proved impractical. The Road Runner inherited its heavy-duty chassis components from Plymouth's police cars and the GTX. The 335-horse-power 383 had the power to achieve the 100-mile-per-hour benchmark.

When engineers completed their job, they had created a car that met performance goals with a base sticker price of $2,896. "They took a bare bones car and put the 383 in it as the base engine and came into the market at a price point where you got a lot of wallop for the buck," exclaims Tom Gale, former Chrysler vice president of design. "In 1968, Road Runners went to 42 percent of volume of B-bodies. If you went to the Lynch Road plant, every second or third car coming down the line was a Road Runner. This got your attention as to how powerful it was as a marketing and merchandising success."

Creating the Road Runner's image was much like Babe Ruth standing at the plate and pointing at center field. If Ruth hadn't hit the home run, he would have looked like a fool; and if the Road Runner's cartoon character image hadn't struck a chord with buyers, a lot of unsold cars would have clogged dealer lots. At that time (and even now), young adult men enjoyed Road Runner cartoons. The unsung, two-legged hero with the distinctive beep-beep voice constantly proved itself to be faster and smarter. The selection of the name Road Runner, and the inclusion of the crafty bird as part of the car's ornamentation, was a grand-slam home run for Plymouth.

During the 1968 model year, the Road Runner began to morph from its stripped-down basic approach to a middle-of-the-road muscle car. A two-door hardtop made a mid-season appearance

The 1969 Plymouth GTX's grille featured a black background with a bright surround. Two red inlayed horizontal bars ran across the middle with a GTX emblem in the center.

135

and sold exceptionally well. Chrysler's product planners took note and made a few adjustments to the 1969 models.

Dodge missed out on the low-priced muscle car game at the beginning of the 1968 season, but it soon added the Super Bee, counterpart to the Road Runner. Dodge didn't use an existing cartoon hero to name its new muscle car. Designers created their own special image—a grinning, fast-moving, helmeted bee with slicks and zoomie headers. The Road Runner and Super Bee's performance—and low price—quickly silenced any laughter coming from those who drove an SS, GTO, or GTA, names that began to sound dated.

Two years earlier Chrysler had been on the outside looking in. Now, the 1968 Plymouth Road Runner and Dodge Super Bee moved into the spotlight. They were lean and mean, meant for boulevard cruising or an occasional street race. They were easy on the pocketbook and hard on the competition. Equally competitive were the GTX and R/T, with standard bucket seats and 375-horsepower, 440-ci engines. These vehicles offered the Mopar buyer a car with special trim and added image, and the Hemi as an option.

Dodge completely restyled the 1968 Dodge Charger. Even though it was built on a basic Coronet B-body platform, it didn't look anything like the Coronet. Dodge designers created an entirely new design without carrying over any of the Coronet's body panels. Its sexy, Coke-bottle

In 1969, Plymouth offered the Road Runner in a convertible body style. Only 2,027 were produced.

shape set it apart from other luxury coupes and its performance was world class. They designed the Charger to look perfectly at home, whether in front of an expensive restaurant or street racing on Woodward Avenue. Dodge created the Charger with the perfect balance of sex appeal and muscle—something rare in the automotive world.

Dodge priced the base 1968 Charger at $3,014. This included standard bucket seats, a 318-ci, V-8 engine, racing-style fuel filler cap, hidden headlights, and sports-car-style instrument panel. And Dodge offered the real bargain in 1968 with the Charger R/T. It listed for $3,480 and included a standard 375-horsepower, 440-ci, Magnum V-8 engine backed by Chrysler's outstanding TorqueFlite automatic or a four-speed manual transmis-

(main) In 1970, Plymouth offered three different engines: the standard 335-horsepower 383 with the 390-horsepower 440 and 426 Hemi being optional. The 375-horsepower 440-ci engine was only available on the 1970 Road Runner Superbird.

(top right) A decal with the little Road Runner bird running at full speed was attached to the front fender of each 1970 Road Runner. The cloud of dust trailing him is the optional Dust Trail stripe that terminated at the quarter panel scoop.

(bottom right) Plymouth installed the 335-horsepower 383 as the base engine in a 1969 Road Runner. The fixture on the bottom of the hood is the optional Air Grabber system.

Plymouth upgraded the exterior of the 1970 Road Runner with a mild facelift. This restyling included a slick set of quarter panel scoops.

In 1970, all four-speed optioned Road Runners and Super Bees were equipped with the beefy Hurst Pistol Grip shifter.

sion (optional at no extra cost). Dodge wrapped the tail of all Charger R/Ts with red, white, or black bumblebee stripes. F70x14 Red Line tires were standard and chrome plated wheels were optional. For a Hemi engine, the buyer was required to start with an R/T and then add an additional $604.75.

In 1968, Chrysler moved from the fringe of the muscle car world to the center. The new Road Runner and Super Bee offered a contemporary level of excitement at a bargain price. The new Charger proved itself when sales jumped by 600 percent over 1967 sales. And the best part? They were all available with the Hemi!

Chrysler's 1968 reinvention of the muscle car set the stage for an even more exciting 1969 model year. Chrysler positioned itself for the muscle-car era's peak years by providing plenty of horsepower at reasonable prices. The Road Runner, GTX, Super Bee, Dodge R/T, and Charger R/T returned with a vengeance in 1969. New and brighter colors covered lightly face-lifted bodies. The Road Runner came in coupe, hardtop, or convertible body styles. The Super Bee added a hardtop version. The engine lineup remained the same until spring when Chrysler released a new engine option package: the most audacious "Six Pack."

Brewers coined the phrase "six-pack" to describe a container that held a half-dozen bottles or cans of beer. The phrase took on new meaning in the spring of 1969 when Dodge announced the arrival of the new Six Pack, a 440-ci, 390-horsepower engine for its Super Bee two-door hardtop and coupe models. In the spring of 1969, Plymouth also offered this engine package in the Road Runner, called "440 6-BBL (barrel)." The Six Pack or Six Barrel refers to the trio of Holley two-barrel carburetors mounted on top of the engine The macho references to an alcoholic beverage or a firearm were not lost on young men coming of age in the late 1960s.

Chrysler didn't simply plop three carburetors on top of a 440 engine to create this package. They installed new, higher-load valve springs to allow higher engine rpm. A low-taper camshaft and flat-face tappets improved durability. Molybdenum-filled top piston rings improved oil economy and engine dura-bility. Chrysler also added chrome-plated valve stems, improved valve guide life, and magnafluxed the connecting rods for high-rpm strength. Chrysler installed a dual-breaker distributor to maintain spark at higher engine rpm. Edelbrock cast the aluminum intake manifold that mounted the three carburetors. The cooling system was upgraded with a viscous-drive fan and a standard heavy-duty cooling package. The power rating for this engine was 390 horsepower at 4,700 rpm, and 490 ft-lb of torque at 3,600 rpm. This was the same torque rating as the Hemi, but at 400 rpm less.

Chrysler only offered two transmissions with the Six Pack: a three-speed TorqueFlite automatic and a four-speed manual with a Hurst shifter. All of the new 440-6BBL Road Runners and Six Pack Super Bees came with 4.10 Dana Sure Grip axles and G70x15 wide-track Red Line tires. These tires were mounted on the same 15x6-inch wheels that were used on the Hemi-equipped Road Runners and Super Bees, but painted black. Unlike on the Hemi, here were no hubcaps with this new option, only chrome lug nuts. "Somebody at Chrysler was really paying attention to what was happening on the street," says Tom Gale. "Can you imagine a car without wheel covers? And yet in that era

For 1971, Dodge Chargers (and Super Bees) were only available in a two-door hardtop body style. This Hemi-powered 1971 Charger is an unrestored 20,000-mile survivor.

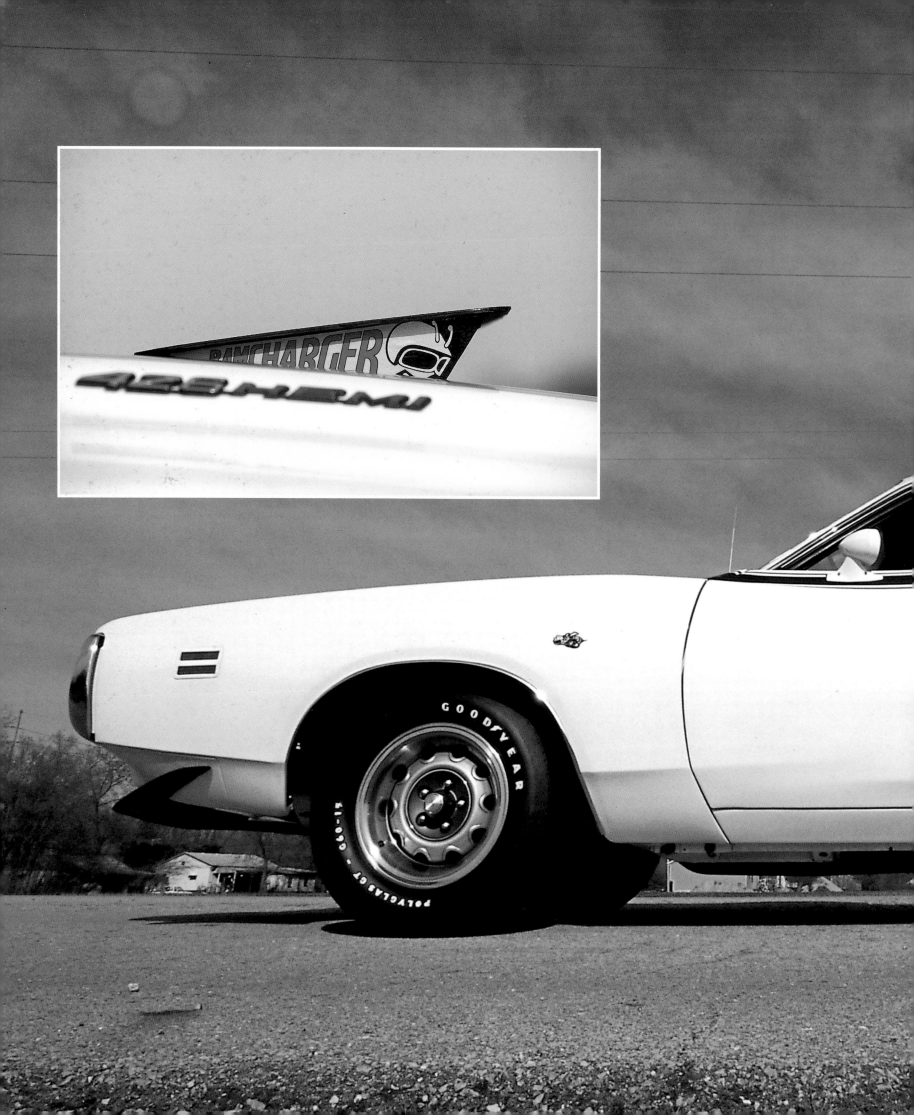

(main) Dodge made the 1971 Super Bee a model of the Charger. This Super Bee is one of 22 produced that year with a Hemi engine. Making this car even more rare is the sunroof option that included a vinyl roof.

(top left) All 1971 Dodge Charger Super Bees (or Charger R/Ts) equipped with a 426 Hemi also came standard with the slick Ramcharger hood scoop. This hood scoop was optional with other engines.

In 1971, Plymouth completely redesigned the Road Runner with this fuselage-style body. Two different hoods were used on 1971 Road Runners. This is the "power dome" version.

This 1971 Road Runner was the last in a long line of muscle cars. The Road Runner lived on in emasculated form, but 1971 was the last year the mighty 440 Six Pack was available.

The 1971 Dodge Super Bee's deck lid was designed with a small spoiler. Added to this Super Bee is the optional rear spoiler that attached to the top of the deck lid.

before specialized wheels, this is what kids did. It was extra stuff you didn't need." In the late 1960s, few car buyers had the extra money for mag wheels. Removing the hubcaps was required when racing at a drag strip. Driving a car on the street without hubcaps gave the impression that the car was meant to race.

Chrysler dropped an image bomb on the competition by equipping these special Road Runners and Super Bees with a fiberglass, lift-off hood. This hood featured the largest and most aggressive functional hood scoop ever installed on a muscle car. All of the hoods were painted flat black and retained by four, competition-type racing pins. Initially, only four, bright, exterior colors were available: green, red, orange, and yellow. The limited choice of such bright colors was another example of Chrysler's in-your-face attitude. Later in the year, Chrysler's full palette of colors could be ordered. Interestingly, the Six Pack option on the Road Runner cost only $462.80, about half the cost of the Hemi option.

The minor changes that Dodge made on the 1969 Charger included a new grille, revised taillights, and small trim changes to the interior. The muscular R/T returned with its standard 440-ci engine and optional Hemi. Dodge made the 318-ci engine optional for 1969 and used a 225-ci slant six as the standard engine. Two new additions were the SE (Special Edition) package and the optional sunroof. The SE option included leather seats, wood-grained steering wheel, wood-grained instrument panel inserts, hood-mounted turn indicators, and pedal trim. The SE package could be added to the standard Charger or the Charger R/T. This would be the first year Dodge offered a sunroof on any of its cars, and the $461.45 price tag included a vinyl-covered roof. Convertible sales in intermediate and full size cars had been falling off, probably due to the option of low-cost, factory air conditioning units on most new cars—and the whims of a fickle public that had lost interest in open cars.

In the late 1960s, auto manufacturers didn't mind the shift away from convertibles, because pending rollover legislation would have required extensive re-engineering and the possible addition of roll bars. Other Charger anomalies in 1969 were the 500 and the Daytona (covered in Chapter 5).

In 1969, Chrysler had reason to celebrate. It had produced 2.2 million units and its market share rose to 18.1 percent. This was up from a 10.3-percent share in 1962. *Motor Trend* magazine named the Road Runner its "Car of the Year" for 1969, the announcement made prior to the release of the Six Pack option. That honor could have gone as easily to the stylish Charger. It is ironic that *Motor Trend* selected the Road Runner in its second year of production. But then again, Pontiac, who's GTO was selected in 1968, had bought more advertising in *Motor Trend*.

Chrysler had to feel good about 1970. Sales were up in 1969 and new cars that had been on the drawing board would soon be in the dealers. This would be the third and final year for the B-body, first introduced in 1968. Facelifts dominated each of the models, with Plymouth coming out as the winner and Dodge in need of help. Plymouth's new front and rear treatments were symmetrical and pleasing to the eye. The 1970 GTX and Road Runner models were fitted with a power-dome hood and small, non-functional scoops stamped into the quarter panels. Dodge's redesign of the Coronet's front end created a decidedly unfriendly "scowling" look. They created this unique look using two oval-shaped, halo bumpers. Dodge also fitted the R/T with large, bolt-on, quarter-panel scoops. Because of the continued decline in convertible sales (only 296 Dodge R/T and 824 Road Runner convertibles were sold), 1970 would be the last year for the B-body drop tops.

Chrysler retained the same engine lineup for its 1970 muscle cars as it had in 1969. The only difference was that the 440-ci Six Pack engine became an option in the GTX and R/T along with the Road Runner and Super Bee. Callouts on the hood indicated this engine. There was no special hood,

When Dodge redesigned the Charger for 1971, they kept the distinctive Coke-bottle shape and rectangular grille from the previous model. This Charger is optioned as a Super Bee with a 440 Six Pack engine and Ramcharger hood.

149

Dodge designers used the latest styling tricks when they designed the 1971 Dodge Charger, including hidden windshield wipers, flush door handles, and ventless door glass.

wheels, or tires. The Six Pack option still cost much less than a Hemi, looked impressive, and ran exceptionally well.

The 1970 Dodge Charger was also treated to a light facelift. The R/T models were fitted with a large, reversed, non-functional scoop on the leading edge of the doors. Dodge removed the center split from the 1969 grille. Like its B-body brothers, the 1970 Charger R/T could be optioned with the powerful Six Pack engine. Sales of the Charger dropped to half of what they were two years earlier, but with sales at 50,000 units, Dodge executives were still pleased.

Plymouth and Dodge introduced their new E-body Barracuda and Challenger in 1970 (covered in chapter 6). Introducing a new model had the effect of a double-edged sword. They increased showroom traffic, but in doing so, may have hurt sales of B-bodies. The 1970 E-bodies were new and exciting, while the B-bodies were in their third year and were looking dated. The design team that had created the exciting E-bodies had also been working on the next generation of B-bodies, scheduled to be released in 1971.

Chrysler not only redesigned, but also restructured, its B-body car lines in 1971. The stage for the redesign was set with the release of the 1970 E-bodied Barracuda and Challenger. Chrysler's designers used the E-body cowl: a modified B-body cowl that allowed for hidden windshield wipers. Designers also smoothly rounded the bodies and used styling and engineering innovations to advance the designs. The restructuring came by way of eliminating all coupe and convertible body styles, and by including the Charger as part of the Coronet series.

In 1971, Plymouth dropped the Belvedere name and used the Satellite name to cover its B-body models, including the Road Runner and GTX. Dodge also renamed the entire B-body line of two-door coupes to Charger, and offered the Super Bee as a Charger model. These new B-bodies featured well-rounded bodies, flush door handles, hidden windshield wipers, and ventless door glass. Unlike the earlier B-bodies, one had to look closely to see the similarities between the new Dodge and Plymouth. Chrysler's styling department once again leapt ahead of the competition.

Chrysler became acutely aware of the pressure the insurance industry was placing on buyers of high-performance cars. Surcharges were added to policies whose holders (usually young males) purchased cars with engines over 350 ci. The accident rate for this age group has always been high, and ownership of a high

The 1973 Road Runner was based on the Plymouth Satellite body. New bumpers, with large bumper guards, were required to meet new federal regulations.

performance vehicle only increased the probability of an accident—presumably, while street racing. To provide a car with plenty of image and decent performance, Chrysler included the 340-ci engine, rated at 275-horsepower, as an option on the Road Runner and Super Bee. The GTX and Charger R/T still came with the 375-horsepower 440. While Six Pack 440 and Hemi were still optional on all of these cars, buyers were hard to find. In 1971, Dodge sold only 5,054 Super Bees and 3,118 Charger R/Ts. Of those, only 85 were equipped with the Hemi. Sales were almost as bad at Plymouth, with only 14,218 Road Runners and 2,942 GTXs delivered in 1971. Plymouth's B-body Hemi sales also totaled 85. The insurance industry and looming emission legislation were smashing muscle cars like watermelons—at a Gallagher concert. "I think Chrysler understood the muscle car world as well as anybody in the late 60s and early 70s," says Tom Gale. "What closed it out in 1971 were emissions. If that hadn't happened, it would have been interesting. Because Chrysler was financially weaker than the others, they couldn't stay in the poker game. They had to walk away from it. It's too bad, because need and desire for performance never went away."

In 1972, the 440 Six Pack and Hemi were no longer available. Nor would the Charger R/T, Super Bee, or GTX be available; only an emasculated version of the Road Runner would continue. Plymouth tried to make the best of a bad situation and offered 340, 400, and 440-ci engine, but sales were only half of that in 1971. The Road Runner languished during the fuel shortages of 1973 and 1974. In 1975, Plymouth added the name and graphics to a Fury. From 1976 through 1980, Plymouth also added the Road Runner name to an option group on the Volare—a sad ending to a once-proud muscle car.

Chrysler engineers didn't invent the muscle car—they redefined it. They added the powerful Hemi engine in 1966 and never looked back. Chrysler's product planners and engineers were smart enough to see what was happening on Detroit's Woodward Avenue and quickly translated that knowledge into showroom-ready racers. The 1968 Road Runner was sheer brilliance. The Six Pack-equipped Road Runners and Super Bees proved that lightning could strike twice. On the street, GTOs and SS Chevelles were toasted golden brown by the phalanx of the powerful Mopars. Sadly, the fingers gripping the windpipe of the muscle car era tightened just as Chrysler introduced some of its finest work. The oxygen feeding the fire disappeared, and so did the cars.

(previous) The Dodge Daytona and Plymouth Superbird were built to comply with NASCAR rules dictating that for a car to be eligible to race, similar cars had to be built for the street.

In 1969, Dodge reconfigured a few of the unsold Charger 500s into winged Daytonas.

*Charger 500, Dodge Daytona,
Plymouth Superbird:*

DESIGNED FOR THE TRACK, BUILT FOR THE STREET

B y 1968, Chrysler had wrung almost all the horsepower it could from the 426 Hemi, and company engineers began looking for other ways to add speed to its NASCAR entries. Chrysler's engineers sought their next challenge in automobile aerodynamics. Reducing high-speed drag is as effective as adding horsepower.

Chrysler's first experiments into this mysterious field involved the 1968 Dodge Charger. While aesthetically beautiful, the Charger lacked aerodynamic efficiency. Its deep-set grille and recessed rear window hurt its high-speed performance. The grille acted like a catcher's mitt, grabbing all the air it could, while the back window created turbulence over the rear of the car. Dodge wanted to showcase this car in NASCAR's race series, but with only two wins for the year, it was a disappointment. Engineers added small spoilers as a quick fix, but they didn't do the job. Chrysler's racing engineer Bob Rodger ordered wind tunnel testing to see what could be done. The tests determined that the new Charger required some major surgery.

In June of 1968, journalists gathered at Chrysler's proving grounds to see the unveiling of a specially modified Dodge Charger. The custom-built 1968 model was scheduled to be released as a 1969 production model named the Charger 500. It addressed the major aerodynamic problems and included a few other trick pieces. This was the first car Chrysler custom built to meet NASCAR's rules.

The numbers "500" were cut out of the bumblebee stripe on the Dodge Charger 500s.

NASCAR's rules encouraged the use of production-based cars in its racing series. In 1965, it banned the Chrysler Hemi engine (along with Ford's SOHC engine) because it was not installed in production cars. Chrysler began offering the engine in its production cars the following year. The rules also required that a company must build at least 500 of a certain model before it could run in any NASCAR race. For this modified Charger to compete in the 1969 series, Dodge had to be ready to build 500 of them for the general public.

Building 500 special cars on the regular Charger production line was impractical. Instead, Creative Industries, a Detroit-area fabrication shop, signed a contract to modify the 500 Charger R/Ts that were to be sold to the public. Chrysler specified fenders and the addition of a Coronet grille mounted flush with the front edge of the hood. This included the Coronet's exposed quad headlights. While not as attractive as the original recessed grille with hidden headlights, this new assembly solved the Charger's frontal aerodynamic difficulties. The solution to the tunneled rear window required an extensive amount of work. Chrysler designed a "plug" that smoothly enclosed the entire rear window area. Because of the length of the original sail panels, this plug covered the forward edge of the deck lid, which required a shortened deck lid. To help move air over the windshield, the A-pillars were covered with smooth stainless covers. To identify each of these special Chargers, the number "500" was cut into the bumblebee stripe on the rear of the car.

Similar to the Charger R/T, the Charger 500 could only be purchased with a 375-horsepower, 440-ci engine or a 425-horsepower Hemi. Also like the Charger R/T, Dodge only offered two transmissions: a four-speed manual and a TorqueFlite automatic. Red Stripe F70x15 tires were standard and White Streak tires were a no-cost option.

Dodge built only 67 Charger 500s with the Hemi engine. *Hot Rod* magazine had scheduled three of them for a road test in their February 1969, issue. One was stolen prior to the evaluation, leaving only two Hemi-powered 500s for *Hot Rod*—a four-speed and a TorqueFlite. In 1969, drag racing's

quarter-mile had become the benchmark for acceleration comparisons, and both Hemi 500s *Hot Rod* tested ran 13-second elapsed times at speeds between 105 and 108 miles per hour.

Ford Motor Company did not sit idly by as Dodge fiddled with the Charger's aerodynamics. Ford employed its wind tunnel to advance its Ford Torino and Mercury Cyclone models. Ford added a flattened, drooped nose to both cars enhancing their ability to slice through the air at high speeds. Ford named its new homologation specials the Torino Talladaga and Mercury Cyclone Spoiler. While both cars were based on the same basic body, the Mercury had slightly better aerodynamics. One of Ford's Torino Talladaga models won the 1969 Daytona 500. Chrysler's aerodynamic work to develop the Charger 500 helped, but did not solve, all of its problems. Chrysler's next step into the brave new world of aerodynamics for NASCAR racing could only be classified as audacious.

Chrysler loved the recognition it got from its NASCAR exploits. NASCAR wins had a halo effect over every car it sold. To make the big investment in the Hemi engine pay off, Chrysler had to one-up Ford with another aerodynamic creation and gain the winning edge.

Three months before losing the 1969 Daytona 500, Chrysler's aerodynamicists and its Special Vehicles Group discussed what could be done to increase the Charger's aerodynamic qualities. The improvements that created the Charger 500 had helped, but the car still had too much front-end

The 1969 Charger 500 was Dodge's first attempt at sweetening a car's aerodynamics for better performance on NASCAR tracks. The modifications on the 500 included a new grille, A-pillar covers, and a new rear window.

When this 1969 Charger 500 was new, no one cared about gas mileage because even premium fuels, like Sunoco 260, were inexpensive.

lift. Engineers determined that a 15-percent reduction in drag would equal an additional 85 horsepower—a goal worth pursuing. Using a Charger 500 as the starting point for a new design, Chrysler aerodynamicist John Pointer and Special Vehicles group member Bob Marcell developed sketches of a Charger with a severely sloped nose and rear wing.

When Dodge Vice President Bob McCurry reviewed the sketches and learned what needed to be done, he only asked if making these changes would ensure wins at the track. Assured that the ungainly looking car would claim the winner's circle, he gave the project the green light, and the team packed up for wind-tunnel testing.

Chrysler used two different wind tunnels to develop the Dodge Daytona. Full-size Chargers were run in the Lockheed-Georgia facility, and 3/8 scale models were run in the Wichita State wind tunnel. The first new nose piece added 9 inches to the front of the car. Engineers eventually lengthened it to 18 inches. This longer nose provided better directional stability and lower drag at high speeds. This large nosepiece also provided enough area for headlights on models destined for the street.

As with the Charger 500, Chrysler had to make 500 Dodge Daytona models available to the general public by September 1, 1969 to be eligible for NASCAR racing. Even as aerodynamic work continued, Creative Industries started gearing up for the production of the components for the race cars and their street versions.

Testing in the wind tunnel determined that to balance the positive effects of the long nose, a sizeable rear wing or spoiler was needed. By raising the wing, they could reduce its size. At 12 inches, a small wing worked effectively, but didn't allow the deck lid to be opened—a feature required on the street versions. Bob Roger and Gary Romberg solved the problem by placing the wing on 23-inch-high uprights, high enough to open the deck lid. At this height, it would receive enough air to produce plenty of downforce at the rear of the car. It turned out that the raised

162

The Dodge Daytona's aerodynamic shape was derived from wind-tunnel testing. The long nose added downforce to the front, and the tall wing added downforce to the rear.

164

The Dodge Charger Daytona had a rear bumblebee-style stripe in red, white, or black. The Daytona's tall wing was also painted to match the stripe.

wing's stanchions produced a secondary benefit of improving straight-line stability, similar to the vertical tail on an airplane.

Corporate politics eventually reared its ugly head. Chrysler's styling staff had not been consulted on the design of the Charger Daytona. As soon as they saw the car, they wanted to make changes. They felt the modified car would hurt the company's image. But McCurry felt confident that the unusually styled car would win races on Sunday—and sell well on Monday. No changes were made to the modified Dodge Daytona.

Early track testing proved Chrysler's aerodynamic theories to be correct. The new elongated nose produced 200 pounds of downforce on the front and the high-mounted rear wing added 600 pounds of downforce at the rear. There was so much downforce that the front tires rubbed the underside of the fenders. John Pointer devised a quick fix for this problem. He cut holes in the tops of the fenders and added small, reversed scoops over the openings. Veteran NASCAR driver Charlie Glotzbach then took the Hemi-powered prototype Dodge Charger Daytona around Chrysler's Chelsea, Michigan proving grounds and recorded speeds of 243 miles per hour.

Dodge introduced the modified Charger 500 as the Dodge Charger Daytona to the press on

April 13, 1969. Creative Industries fabricated a nosepiece from fiberglass and the headlight doors were traced on its surface with black tape. Simple posts supported the hastily fabricated fiberglass rear wing instead of the streamlined fairings used on the production versions. Those in attendance couldn't help but notice the unusual reversed scoops on the tops of the front fenders. The press, and even many of the competitors, thought there was more to them than just "tire clearance." The press loved the unusual-looking Daytona, as did members of the general public, who quickly placed their orders.

Creative Industries was required to ship production versions to dealers by September 1, 1969. Initially, Creative Industries built only two or three cars per day. Eventually, production increased to 20 cars per day and within three months, the company had assembled 503 cars. A parallel program manufactured components that allowed any competitor with a Charger 500 race car to convert it into a Charger Daytona. At a list price of only $3,993.00, the Charger Daytona was the bargain of the century. A big-block 1969 Corvette sold for about the same amount.

Dodge offered only two engines in the Daytona: a 375-horsepower 440, and the optional Hemi for $648.20. Because of the limited airflow to the radiator caused by the Daytona's extended nose,

Chrysler dominated NASCAR in the 1960s and early 1970s, first with the powerful Hemi engines and then with the radical aerodynamically styled Dodge Charger Daytonas and Plymouth Superbirds.

Because of the small grille opening under the Superbird's pointy nose, airflow to the radiator was limited. For this reason, air conditioning could not be added.

While the Superbird's nose looks similar to the one on the Dodge Daytona, it's completely different. The only interchangeable parts are the headlight doors.

Dodge eliminated air conditioning from the option list. All Charger Daytona models were marked with a wide band stripe across the rear of the car in black, red, or white. Dodge painted the entire wing and vertical supports the same color as the stripe. On the quarter panel, Dodge cut the letters DAYTONA out of the stripe so they showed through in contrasting body color.

The Charger Daytona proved to be an excellent performer on the track. At its high-speed debut at Talladega, Alabama in September of 1969, it became the fastest stock car in history by taking the pole for the Talladega 500 with a speed of 199.466 miles per hour. Richard Brickhouse won the race driving a Charger Daytona, but it was a hollow victory for Dodge— all the Ford teams withdrew from competition, citing unsafe conditions due to the rough

The aerodynamically sleek Dodge Daytona and Plymouth Superbird dominated the NASCAR tracks. Because of their superiority, they were "legislated" out of competition.

surface of the track. David Pearson won the 1969 NASCAR season title in a Torino Talladega. Dodge's fortunes improved in 1970 when Bobby Isaac won the NASCAR championship at the wheel of his number 71, K&K Insurance-sponsored Charger Daytona.

The 1969 Charger Daytona became the most outrageous and infamous of the Dodge Chargers. Estimates tagged the extra cost per car at $1,500, with the total cost of the entire Daytona project at one million dollars. The Charger Daytona was Chrysler's innovative approach to building an unbeatable race car for NASCAR competition.

1970 Road Runner Superbird

The biggest problem with the Dodge Daytona was that Richard Petty didn't get one. When Petty first heard about the Dodge Daytona, he asked his sponsors at Plymouth if they had plans to give him a new car to compete with the Daytona. Because Petty had been winning a lot of races, Plymouth felt there was no reason to give him a better car. They intended for him to continue driving the Plymouth with which he had been winning races. But Petty wanted a Dodge Daytona. He was told that he couldn't have a Dodge because he was a "Plymouth man." Petty knew that the winged Daytona was superior to his Road Runner. A frustrated Petty tried again, and was given a final "no" from Plymouth—so he left and went to Ford.

For the 1969 NASCAR season, Richard Petty drove a Petty Blue Ford Talledaga and won nine races. Halfway through the 1969 season, a representative from Plymouth approached him and said, "Look, we're going to build a Plymouth [Superbird]. How long is your contract?" Petty said, "You build a Superbird and we'll run for you next year."

The leading edge of the Dodge Daytona's nose was slightly lower than that of the Plymouth Superbird, giving the Dodge slightly more downforce.

Plymouth scrambled to build a winged car of its own in order to lure Petty back. To comply with new NASCAR rules, Plymouth was required to make 1,500 cars available to the public. The overwhelming reception of the Dodge Daytona convinced Plymouth's marketing staff that the Superbird would sell well. They quickly forecasted 1,850 units: 480 in the Eastern sales district, 385 in the Central, 270 in the Western, 338 in the Midwest, and 377 in the Southern sales district.

Creative Industries, the builders of the Dodge Daytona, received the contract for the Superbird. Initially, it looked like a simple job of adapting the Daytona's nose and wing to a 1970 Road Runner. But it wasn't that simple. While the Superbird's additional nose and wing looked similar to the Dodge Daytona's, they were all unique. Only the headlight doors were directly exchangeable. The formidable task of assembling the Superbird was made even more difficult with the imposition of a completion deadline of January 1, 1970. On this date, new federal regulations went into effect that would have made the Superbird's headlight configuration illegal.

All Superbirds began life at Chrysler's Lynch Road assembly plant as standard 1970 Road Runners. The color selection for the core vehicles was limited to Alpine White, Petty Blue (also referred to as Corporate Blue), Lemon Twist, Tor-Red, Burnt Orange Metallic, Vitamin C Orange, Limelight, and Blue Fire Metallic. The interior came in black or white. From the assembly plant, the cars were trucked to Chrysler's Clairponte facility where the Road Runners were transformed into Superbirds.

Chrysler's winged Dodge Daytonas and Plymouth Superbirds were the most audacious cars ever built during the muscle car era.

When creating the Superbird, Plymouth designers used 1970 Dodge Coronet front fenders and hoods as their starting point. Creative Industries designed the nose. This is the same Detroit-area shop that did the modifications to the Dodge Daytona.

The mirrors of the NASCAR competitors would only see this view of a Dodge Daytona for a short time before it blew by.

Plymouth fitted each Superbird with 15-inch-diameter Rallye wheels that mounted wide Goodyear F60x15 raised white letter tires.

The Road Runner also had airflow problems over its roof. The double-curved back window looked attractive, but it disturbed the air over the rear of the car. Creative Industries designed a rear window cap similar to the one used on the Dodge Daytona. To save time, Plymouth specified a black vinyl top on all Superbirds to cover the cap's unsightly edges. Engineers also added A-pillar covers like those on the Dodge Daytona.

Blending of the Superbird's special nose required the use of Dodge Coronet fender and hood components. The hood required an extension to match the nose. Although designer input was not considered in creation of the Dodge Daytona, Plymouth's design staff left their signature on the finished product. The extension of the hood's center peak down onto the nose piece was no doubt a suggestion from Plymouth's designers. And unlike the Daytona's nose, which had a screened opening on its leading edge, the Superbird's leading edge was trimmed with a small black rubber molding with a screened opening below. Turn signals were installed on each side of that opening. To break up the expanse of the top surface of the Superbird's nose, Plymouth designers added backed-out panels that covered the headlight doors. A circular Road Runner/Superbird decal was added to the driver's side headlight door. The Superbird used the same fender-top reversed scoops as the Dodge Daytona to solve tire clearance problems.

The Superbird also used a high-mounted rear wing. Its die-cast vertical stabilizers had a wider base than those on the Daytona and featured a pronounced, rearward rake. All Superbird wings

Plymouth blacked out the front of the Superbird's extended nose. They added a Road Runner Superbird decal on the driver's side headlight door. The leading edge of the Superbird's nose was trimmed with a black rubber strip.

and vertical supports were painted body-color. On the side of each vertical support, Plymouth placed a large Road Runner/Superbird decal similar to the one on the headlight door, and a large PLYMOUTH decal was placed on the quarter panel. The Superbird's overall aerodynamics proved not as efficient as those of the Charger Daytona. Design compromises, due to the configuration of the rear window and the nose height, were cited as the reasons.

Plymouth specified a 440-ci engine with a single, four-barrel carburetor rated at 375 horsepower as the Superbird's standard engine. This was the only time that particular engine could be ordered in a 1970 (or any) Road Runner. Plymouth listed the 390-horsepower 440 with the six-barrel configuration of three two-barrel Holley carburetors as an optional engine, along with the powerful 426 Hemi. Unlike the standard 1970 Road Runner, Plymouth placed no external engine identification badges on the Superbird. Plymouth also eliminated certain options: the Air Grabber hood, air conditioning, and because of the unique rear window, a rear defroster and seat speaker were also not available. Required options on the Superbird included hood pins, the performance axle package, power steering, and power disc brakes.

Plymouth's marketing and sales departments had seen how fast the Dodge Daytona moved and anticipated the same for the new Superbird. But they overestimated the market for this unique car. Many Superbird models remained trapped in dealer showrooms, victims of their own high price and exotic nature.

Chrysler set its sights on additional winged cars with the release of the new 1971 B-body. A pointed nose and a tall wing, similar to those on the Charger Daytona and Superbird, were on the drawing board. But Chrysler cut its racing budget, and NASCAR, which feared an onslaught of impractical road cars, ruled that any winged cars would be limited to a 305-ci engines. NASCAR wanted to provide a racing series for standard production passenger cars and Chrysler's exotic winged cars were out of step with that goal. This change ended the saga of the most audacious passenger cars ever built.

When equipped with a Hemi engine, Dodge Daytonas were fitted with 15-inch-diameter wheels that mounted the small dog-dish hub caps.

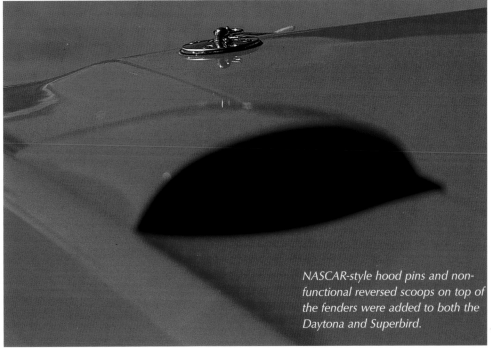

NASCAR-style hood pins and non-functional reversed scoops on top of the fenders were added to both the Daytona and Superbird.

Though never quite as popular as Plymouth's 'Cuda, the Dodge Challenger developed a devoted following of its own.

E-BODY

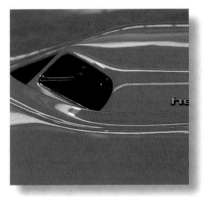

Few people could foresee the quantum leap that Chrysler took in 1970 by creating an entirely new pony car. Even though Ford cracked the pony car code, Chrysler extracted its DNA and when it created the E-body. The new Barracuda and Challenger contained that rare combination of slinky sex appeal and macho muscle.

Mustang set the standard for the iconic pony car proportions: a short rear deck and a long hood. When Chevrolet released the Camaro in 1967, it featured the same proportions. Both Mustangs and Camaros featured smoothly rounded sides, wide grille openings with a deeply set grilles, and slender bumpers. The Camaro had the drawback of being built around the Nova's bulky cowl, which resulted in a higher hood than Chevrolet's stylists wanted for such a sporty car. Ford offered the Mustang in three body styles: coupe, convertible, and fastback, while the Camaro offered only a coupe and convertible. Both offered a wide selection of engines and a lengthy list of options. For these reasons, they were hot sellers.

When the 1970 models were introduced in the fall of 1969, Ford gave the Mustang a facelift and, due to a lengthy UAW strike, the all-new 1970 Camaro was nowhere to be seen. When it finally appeared in the spring of 1970, the sleek new body had the appearance of a European car. Chevrolet created a new platform for the Camaro and stylists had the freedom to explore new design concepts, but retained the popular long-nose, short-deck styling. In a conservative move,

Plum Crazy was one of the high-impact colors available for the 1970 Plymouth 'Cuda. It contrasts well with the white interior and white hockey stick stripe.

Chevrolet produced only one body style for the new Camaro: a fastback coupe. Chevrolet scratched the convertible because of upcoming government rollover standards and the public's unwillingness to buy convertibles. In addition to the Mustang and the Camaro in 1970, Chrysler had to contend with the Mercury Cougar, Pontiac Firebird, and AMC Javelin. With all these magnificent cars, 1970 would turn out to be the greatest year in pony car history.

The New E-Body

The strength of the pony car market in the mid-1960s encouraged Chrysler to give the next generation Barracuda its own unique platform—the E-body. Work on the 1970 model began as early as 1967. To compete with the upscale Mercury Cougar, Chrysler gave Dodge its own version that would ultimately be called the Challenger.

One of the first design parameters for Chrysler's new E-body models was the ability to install all of Chrysler's engines, including the Hemi. The engine compartment had to be big enough so those ordering the 440-ci engine would not be penalized with a restricted option list. To make this possible, Chrysler designers started with a modified B-body cowl. Structurally, the cowl is the strongest and most important component of an automobile body. In addition, the cowl also houses the steering column, brake booster, heater and air conditioner, and windshield wipers. Using the derivative B-body cowl automatically gave the new E-body a wider track and allowed the use of the existing K-member. With the cowl in place, Chrysler's package engineers set about to determine wheelbase, passenger seating, belt line, greenhouse, and door openings—all from the cowl. Once the package drawings were completed, the styling groups worked their magic.

John Herlitz was directed the design of the new Barracuda's exterior in the Plymouth studio. His vision was to pull the quarters as high as possible while making the roof as low as possible. The Challenger also featured a raised quarter panel and low roofline. This created an aggressive, hunched forward look that emphasized the Barracuda's long front end. Chief Dodge Designer Bill Brownlie wanted a wider body accented by a pronounced character line down the side.

Even though the Barracuda and Challenger looked similar, they shared no external sheet metal and rode on different wheelbases. During a design review the Challenger's wheelbase was extended to 110 inches, compared to the Barracuda's 108-inch wheelbase. This small stretch was an easy change, helped differentiate the cars, and only required a new floor pan. This additional wheelbase and longer overall length of the Challenger resulted in a slight increase in rear seat room, as well. In addition to the overall size, subtle differences made the two new E-bodies noticeably distinguishable from one another, but they still had an underlying Chrysler family resemblance.

Automotive designers always incorporate the latest in technological and material advances into their designs. Curved side glass first appeared on a Chrysler-built car in 1966. Chrysler's designers use this curved glass to their advantage when creating the highly rounded E-body shapes. They also incorporated flush door handles, ventless door glass, and hidden windshield wipers. They wanted a full Endura front bumper similar to the GTO, but cost considerations nixed the idea. They added the Elastomeric bumper option that provided for body-colored bumpers. It wasn't as elegant as a full Endura nose, but it integrated well with the front end design.

Plymouth's designers equipped the Barracuda with a pair of seven-inch headlamps, while the Challenger used quad lamps. Hidden headlamps were never a consideration. Dodge designers rounded the top of Challenger's wheel openings and added a pronounced flare, while the Barracuda's were flatter on top with a mild flare. In the rear, the Challenger featured a full-width taillight, while the Barracuda had its taillights at each end of a recessed panel. The differences between the two models even extended to the side marker lights: long and thin on the Barracuda, wider on the Challenger. Common to both cars were the two small vertical rear bumper guards that masked the rear spring mount on each side.

Both the 1970 Barracuda and Challenger offered basic and performance models to suit every taste and pocketbook. Plymouth continued with the 'Cuda as its performance model and Dodge added its traditional R/T label to the hottest Challengers. Before the end of the 1970 model year, both car lines would build a special small-block version—the AAR 'Cuda and the Challenger T/A— designed to suit the SCCA's Trans-Am rule makers. This wide selection of E-body models and powerful engines gave buyers many choices when selecting a distinctive muscle car.

Chrysler only designed a coupe and a convertible for its 1970 E-bodies. A fastback would have added cost and complexity. Chrysler offered some of the most dazzling colors ever seen on an automobile. In addition to being visually stunning, Chrysler's inventive product planners gave them memorable names like Lime Light, Top Banana, and Tor-Red. Accenting the 'Cuda's quarter panels were optional black "hockey stick" tape stripes. These stripes terminated at the rear edge of the quarter panel with an engine size callout (340, 383, or 440, or HEMI). Dodge added standard rear bumblebee stripes to the Challenger R/T. These stripes were Green, Bright Blue, Bright Red, Black, or White, depending on body color, and could be deleted. Dodge also offered a side tape stripe on the 1970 Challenger R/T. It ran the full length of the car along the character line and could be ordered in White, Black, Blue, Green, or Red. A small "R/T" logo was cut out of the stripe on the front fender.

Both 1970 E-bodies were available with a similar selection of performance engines. The base engine for the performance-based 'Cuda and Challenger R/T was the 335-horsepower 383. 'Cuda buyers also had the choice of a 275-horsepower, 340-ci engine as a no-cost option instead of the standard 383. This engine could also be ordered on the Challenger, but not one with the R/T option. The 'Cuda or R/T buyer could specify the 375-horsepower, 440-ci engine for an additional $130.55, the highest horsepower engine available if a buyer wanted air conditioning and automatic speed control. For $249.55, buyers could order the three-two-barrel-equipped 440, rated at 390-horsepower. This was an improved version of the engine offered in the 1969 Six Pack Super Bee and 6BBL Road Runner. For durability, Chrysler beefed up the connecting rods, coated the cam with Lubrite to prevent scuffing, and increased tension on the oil control rings. They also replaced the Edelbrock aluminum intake manifold with a cast iron version. This option also included all of the Hemi's upgraded chassis and cooling components. The 425-horsepower Hemi could be added for an additional $871.45. In addition to prestige, the Hemi offered 35 more horsepower than the Six Pack 440 as well as a standard Shaker Hood on the 'Cuda (Challenger R/T buyers had to pay an additional $97.30 for a Shaker Hood). The Shaker Hood was an option (listed as the "Fresh Air Hood"), with either 440 engine at the beginning of the model year, and eventually optional with any 'Cuda or R/T engine. In 1970, there were two transmission choices with either performance E-body: a four-speed manual with a Hurst Pistol Grip shifter or a Torqueflite automatic.

Chrysler's Trans-Am E-bodies

Plymouth's AAR 'Cuda and Dodge's Challenger T/A were the most unique of the 1970 E-body performance packages. Plymouth derived its "AAR" name from Dan Gurney's All American Racers

and the Challenger "T/A" name came from the SCCA's (Sports Car Club of America) Trans-Am racing series. These cars were brought to market so Chrysler could compete head-to-head with the Z-28 Camaro and Boss 302 Mustang in Trans-Am. According to the SCCA's formula, Chrysler had to build 2,800 Barracudas and 2,500 Challengers with an eligible engine in order to compete in the Trans-Am series. The SCCA also required a displacement of 305 ci or less from a stock block with an original maximum displacement of 350 ci. In race form, Chrysler's bulletproof 340-ci engine was de-stroked to 303.8 ci. These engines developed more than 460 horsepower and revved in excess of 8,000 rpm.

The production AAR 'Cuda and Challenger T/A received engines that were significantly upgraded from standard production engines. The list of upgrades was comprehensive, including stronger engine blocks capable of accepting four-bolt main bearing caps, specially machined cylinder heads, longer pushrods with adjusters, special offset rocker arms, heavy-duty snap rings in the hydraulic lifters, additional oiling grooves in the rocker shafts, and aluminum intake manifolds that mounted three Holley two-barrel carburetors. Chrysler provided a standard 8 3/4-inch Sure Grip rear axle with 3.55:1 gears, with an optional 3.91:1 available.

Chrysler installed a unique exhaust system on the AAR and T/A that featured side exits in front of the rear tires. They did this to simulate a Trans-Am race car's exhausts. This system required dual transverse-flow mufflers and a special set of pipes with chrome plated megaphone tips. This system could not clear the ramps on the transport trucks, so Chrysler shipped the exhaust pipes and chrome tips in the trunk of the car for dealer installation. Because of the car's forward rake, the mufflers and pipes could be seen from the rear, so Chrysler painted them black.

Chrysler fine-tuned a suspension package to suit the AAR and T/A's road race image. Up front,

Hemi 'Cudas, in both 1970 and 1971, were equipped with the Shaker hood scoop as standard equipment. A lever at the bottom of the instrument panel controlled the opening in the front of the scoop.

For 1971, Plymouth changed the front end of the 'Cuda by adding quad headlights and the "cheese grater" grille. This 'Cuda is optioned with the body-colored elastomeric front bumper and grille.

The 1970 Dodge Challenger R/T was available in either hardtop or convertible body styles. The R/T came with a standard bumblebee stripe that could be replaced with an optional side stripe.

The 1970 Challenger R/T came with a standard set of all-vinyl high-back bucket seats and the Rallye Cluster instrument panel. A center console was an extra-cost option.

The 1970 Dodge Challenger R/T used a special hood with a raised center dome and twin simulated air scoops. The Shaker hood scoop was an extra-cost option on the Challenger R/T, even with a Hemi.

If there was any doubt which engine was powering the 'Cuda that handed you your derriere at the drag strip, the optional giant "billboard" tape graphics dispelled any doubts.

Chrysler installed heavy-duty Hemi torsion bars and a large (.95 diameter) sway bar. In the rear, a special set of 4 1/2 leaf rear springs were installed. These springs had an additional arch that raised the rear of the car to provide rear tire clearance and extra road clearance for the side-exiting exhaust. Chrysler also added a rear sway bar to the AAR 'Cuda and Challenger T/A, the only E-body in 1970 to be so equipped. In 1971, this rear sway bar became part of the optional Rallye suspension. Adding to the nose-down rake provided by the rear springs were "big 'n' little" Goodyear raised-white-letter Polyglas tires. As standard equipment on the AAR and T/As, Chrysler installed E60x15 tires in the front, with G60x15 tires in the rear. This combination of springs and tires gave all AARs and T/As an exceptionally aggressive stance.

Chrysler added 15x7-inch wheels to support the wide tires used on the AAR 'Cudas and Challenger T/As. The AAR 'Cudas were fitted with Rallye wheels, while the Challenger T/As used a black painted steel wheel with a center cap and trim ring; Rallye wheels were available as an option. The 15-inch wheels required special front fenders featuring a rolled inner flange for extra tire clearance when turning. All AARs and T/As came standard with a power-assisted brake system with 11-inch-diameter front-disc brakes and 11-inch drums on the rear. Chrysler offered a four-wheel disc brake package as a dealer-installed option. Also available as a dealer-installed option on the AARs

and T/As was a fast-ratio steering with a 12:1 ratio. The standard manual steering had a ratio of 24:1, and the optional power assisted steering had a ratio of 16:1.

Chrysler installed a small black ABS plastic rear spoiler on both the AAR and T/A as standard equipment. This unique spoiler could not be ordered as an option on any other production 'Cuda or Challenger. The rear wing spoiler, optional on all 'Cudas and Challengers, could not be ordered on either the AAR or T/A. Also available were dealer-installed front "chin whisker" spoilers. Dealer-installed components reduced assembly line complexity and manufacturing cost. Throughout the 1950s-1970s, the manufacturers tried to pass on as much assembly work as possible to the dealers.

Chrysler designed a special fiberglass hood with an integral scoop for the Challenger T/A and AAR 'Cuda, painted flat black top and bottom. These functional hoods provided cold air to the three Holley carburetors below. The AAR's hood featured a stylish reverse NACA-style scoop cut into the front of the hood, while the T/A's scoop was a more traditional style. Chrysler raised the T/A's scoop opening above the hood's surface to increase its effectiveness. Unlike the 1969 1/2 lift-off hoods, the T/A and AAR hoods were hinged at the rear and used low-tension springs to hold the hood open. They were held closed by NASCAR-style hood pins.

Chrysler trimmed each model with its own unique style of matte black side stripes. The AAR 'Cuda's dramatic strobe stripes ran the full length of the body. Created by Plymouth designer Jeff Godshall, the stripe segments started out wide and got progressively thinner toward the rear of the car. The stripe terminated the rear edge of the quarter panel with a "'Cuda" decal and a red, white, and blue AAR shield. The Challenger T/A's stripe started at the leading edge of the front fender and flowed back along the belt line. Its rear edge terminated at the C-pillar and was cut to match the angle of the pillar's leading edge. Cut into the stripe on the front fender was a "T/A" logo. Directly below the T/A on the stripe Chrysler added a "340 SIX PACK" decal. Dodge designers also placed a

The 1970 'Cuda hockey stick stripes terminated at the end of the quarter panel with either the callout of the engine's cubic-inch measurement (340, 383, or 440), or simply HEMI in the case of the Hemi.

All Hemi-optioned 1970 'Cudas received an extra-heavy-duty suspension with torsion bars up front and parallel leafs in the rear. Plymouth only built 14 Hemi-powered 'Cuda convertibles in 1970.

Everything about the 'Cuda projected power, style, and speed. The Hurst Pistol Grip shifter exemplified the fact that Plymouths designer's left no small detail unattended to meet the car's image objectives.

white "Challenger T/A" decal on the right side of the rear spoiler. Stripes on the regular production 'Cuda and Challenger could be deleted, but not on the T/A or AAR.

The interior colors and designs for the AAR and T/A were the same as the standard 'Cuda and R/T, including a wide selection of seat coverings, from hound's tooth cloth to leather. Bucket seats were the most popular, but many cars were built with a split bench seat. Chrysler restricted the T/A and AAR models from being equipped with air conditioning, extra heavy-duty suspension, cruise control, and luggage racks. Vinyl tops could be added, but only in black.

Chrysler's 1970 Challenger T/A and 'Cuda AAR were great-running cars. In showroom trim, they could buzz through the quarter mile in the low 14-second range at 100 miles per hour. Their excellent brake package, outstanding suspension, and wide tires gave them superior stopping and cornering capabilities.

The T/A Challenger and AAR 'Cuda are highly collectible, partly because they were only offered one year—the year that they participated in the Trans-Am series. Ads for the 1971 Challenger showed a photo of a Challenger in T/A trim, but none were produced. Production of the two models totaled 5,124 units.

Chrysler's new 1970 E-bodies were instant hits. They offered the pony car customer the ability to order a personalized car with a wide selection of powerful engines, heavy-duty options, and vivid colors. The new 'Cudas and

Challenger R/Ts blurred the line between muscle car and pony car. A Hemi- or Six Pack-equipped 'Cuda or Challenger R/T could easily bitch-slap any big block Camaro or Mustang on the street.

1971 E-Bodies

Only a few changes were made to the 1971 Barracuda and Challenger exterior, and the engine line-up was revised. Chrysler knew it had a good thing going and didn't tamper with the success in 1970 of the E-bodies. When the 1971 E-bodies were released, the nifty Trans-Am-styled AAR 'Cuda and T/A Challenger were no longer available. Chrysler had decided not to return to the SCCA's racing series and didn't need to build a special line of production cars. The insurance industry was also sucking the oxygen out of the muscle car's lungs by making big block cars exorbitantly expensive to insure. Chrysler also knew that several engines they were offering would not pass the new emission regulations. When Chrysler saw the muscle car phenomenon spinning down, their interest in pumping money into a shrinking line of cars diminished, as well. But Chrysler managers refused to exit on a sour note. They put an exclamation point on the

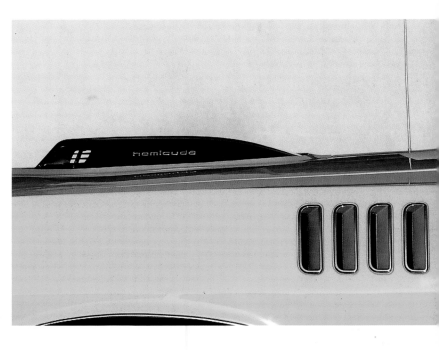

For 1971, the outrageous 'Cuda became an even more outrageous fish, thanks to the addition of these non-functioning gills.

If this 1971 Hemi 'Cuda looks familiar, it's because it's the car that Don Johnson selected as the prototype for his ride in the Nash Bridges television series. Only 7 Hemi 'Cuda convertibles were built in 1971.

A pair of road lights were mounted under the front bumper of all 1970 and 1971 'Cudas. The switch for these lamps was located on the lower end of the instrument panel to the left of the steering wheel.

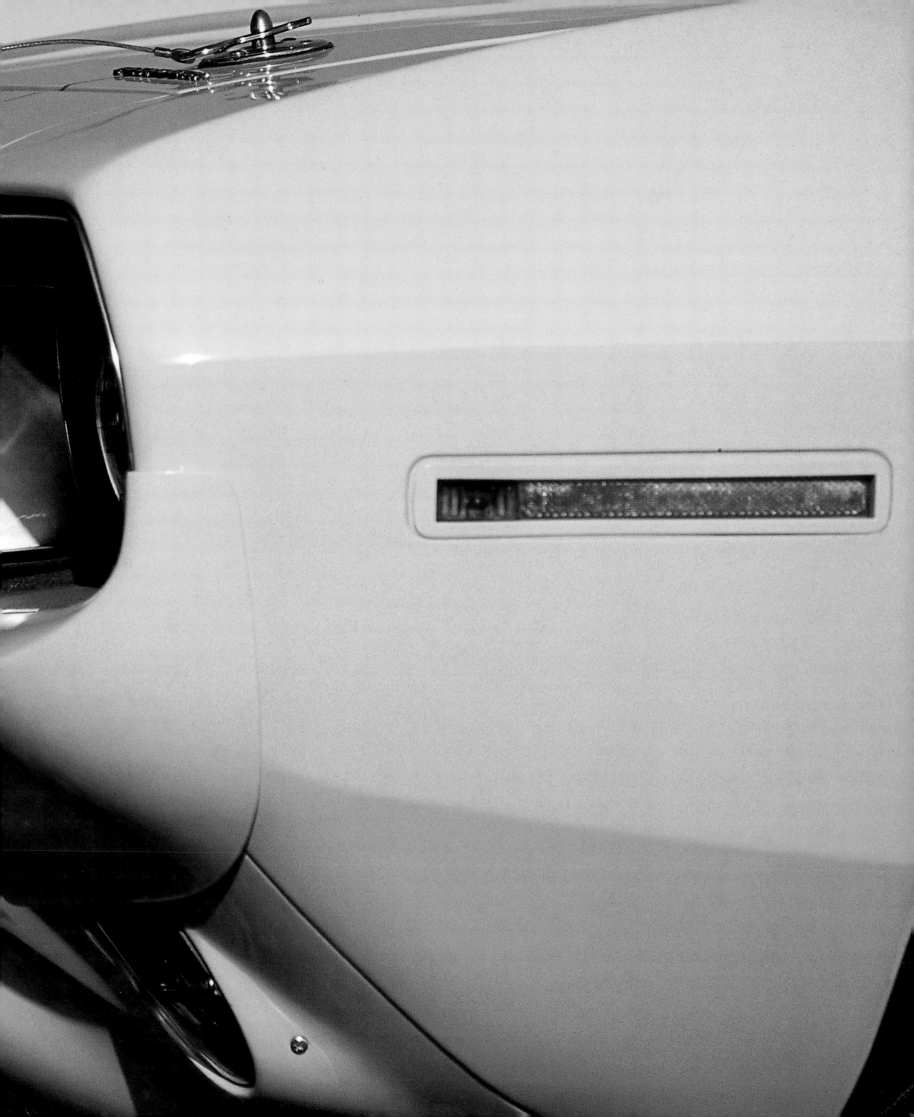

To compete in the SCCA's 1970 Trans-Am series, Dodge was required to build a specified amount of cars similarly equipped to those being raced. Dodge created the Challenger T/A with a 290-horsepower 340-ci engine for this series.

muscle car era by producing two of the most stylish and powerful pony cars ever built.

In 1971, Plymouth returned with a mildly updated 'Cuda in both convertible and coupe body styles. Designers fitted a new grille with three distinct rectangular openings on each side, affectionately known as a "cheese grater." Plymouth painted the grille surround in body color or Argent silver, depending on the car's exterior color. Designers dropped the single headlights from the 1970 Barracudas and 'Cudas in favor of a new quad-headlight arrangement. Plymouth added four Argent-silver colored, non-functional louvers to the front fenders on 'Cuda models. These ornaments were quickly nicknamed "gills." Plymouth's most dramatic addition to the 1971 'Cuda was the addition of optional "billboard" tape accents. These 82 3/8-inch-long, 20-inch-high tape accents were only available in white or black. They extended from the center of the door to the end of the quarter panel. At the leading edge, Plymouth's designers added engine size callouts for all engines except the Hemi, where they added the word "HEMI." These were the most audacious stripes ever added to a production car.

The 1971 Dodge Challenger also received a light facelift. Dodge designers fitted a new grille with a small center split. They specified Argent silver paint for the standard Challenger and black for the R/T's grille. They also revised the Challenger's taillights. The full-width 1970 taillight made way for a pair of elongated taillights with integrated backup lights and a Challenger emblem centered between them. Dodge designers added a pair of quarter-panel scoops to the sides of the 1971 Challenger R/T models. They mounted these non-functional scoops in front of the rear wheel opening and painted them body color. Dodge also revised the side stripes for the R/T to an abbreviated style similar to the 1970 Challenger T/A. While Dodge offered a Challenger convertible in 1971, it was no longer available with the R/T option, which could only be purchased in hardtop.

The EPA began tightening a noose that could be felt under the hoods of Chrysler's 1971 E-bodies. Some engines were no longer available, and the compression ratios on others were reduced, resulting in lower horsepower.

196

Chrysler used its extensive unitized-body experience when it designed the 1970 E-body Plymouth Barracuda and Dodge Challenger. The front suspension and engine were cradled in a large steel K-member that added rigidity to the front end.

Chrysler eliminated the 375-horsepower 440 and the 335-horsepower 383 from the option list, and made the 300-horsepower 383 engine the standard. power plant for the 'Cuda and Challenger R/T. The 275-horsepower 340 ci engine could be substituted for the 383 at no charge. The 440 Six Pack, now rated at 385-horsepower, and Hemi, which retained its 425-horsepower rating, were still options.

In 1971, it took a brave person with lots of cash or a fool to buy a big block E-body—or any kind of muscle car. The police were cracking down on drive-in cruising and street racing. The astronomical

Buyers of 1970 Plymouth Barracudas had a wealth of options from which to choose. The basic Barracuda could be fully dressed-out with luxury options or the buyer could opt for the 'Cuda with its long list of high-performance engines.

insurance rates made buyers take a hard look at any car with an big engine. Suddenly, sitting in a drive-in restaurant and street racing didn't seem so important, clearly evidenced by the drop in sales of both performance E-bodies. In 1970, Plymouth sold 17,792 'Cudas and Dodge sold 18,512 Challenger R/Ts. In 1971, those numbers dropped to 5,607 and 5,588 respectively. In 1970, Plymouth sold 666 'Cudas equipped with the Hemi engine and in 1971, only 115 were sold. The numbers were equally depressing for the Challenger R/T, with 355 Hemi models sold in 1970 and 71 sold in 1971. The E-bodies would hang on for another couple of years in hope that Chrysler could at least recoup its investment.

Dodge juggled the engine lineup for 1971 to help buyers of new Challenger R/Ts with their insurance premiums. The R/T's standard 383-ci engine was reduced in horsepower from 335 to 300 and the 275-horsepower 340-ci engine became a no-cost option in place of the 383.

1972 – 1974 E-bodies

In 1972, Plymouth still marketed 'Cudas, but Dodge replaced the Challenger R/T with the "Rallye." The biggest engine available for either car displaced 340 ci and developed 240 horsepower. The

Plymouth offered a wide variety of engines in the 1970 'Cuda, ranging from 340-ci to 426-ci. Each engine was matched with transmission and chassis components for performance and durability. This 'Cuda has a 440 Six Pack engine under the hood.

(main) Chrysler used its extensive unitized-body experience when it designed the 1970 E-body Plymouth Barracuda and Dodge Challenger. The front suspension and engine were cradled in a large steel K-member that added rigidity to the front end.

Plymouth offered a wide range of engines in the 1970 'Cudas. This one is equipped with a 440-ci 390-horsepower engine with a Shaker hood scoop.

The Dodge Challenger was built with a 110-inch wheelbase (two inches longer than the Barracuda). The aggressive stance on this 1971 Challenger R/T is due to the F-70x15 white letter tires that are required with the Hemi engine.

Dodge designers made a small revision to the1971 Challenger RTs grille and then painted it black.

Dodge fitted the 1971 Challenger R/T with a pair of non-functional scoops in front of the rear wheels. The R/T's side stripes end at the rear edge of the quarter window.

The 1971 Dodge Challenger R/Ts received a large R/T decal on the hood. The twin scoop hood was again standard on the R/T with any engine, but the Shaker hood was an option.

monstrous power was gone, but in 1971, so was the interest in muscle cars. The new generation of buyers didn't care as much about horsepower and performance. And the generation that had grown up with muscle cars had now grown out of them. They were tired of paying high prices for insurance and getting tickets for street racing. Raising a family and buying a house took precedence.

The reduction in sales sealed the E-body's fate. Between 1972 and 1974, Chrysler's designers would make only small changes to the grille and taillights to ensure that the cars looked different from the previous year. Most of the money put into cars was to meet federal emission and crash standards. The Shaker hoods of 1970 and 1971 gave way to electronic ignitions, hardened valve seats, and lower compression ratios so the cleaner-running engines could run unleaded gas. Also no longer available were the wide 60-series tires on 15-inch wheels. Tape stripes were changed annually to help customers identify each year's model. Adapting to the government's standard that bumpers actually "bump" and prevent damage meant large rubber bumper guards in 1973 and even larger ones in 1974. In 1974, Ford released its new, smaller Mustang II to great fanfare, and Chrysler called it quits on the E-body.

When Chrysler entered the pony car field with its new 'Cuda and Challenger in 1970, it met the veteran pony cars head on. Not only did Chrysler match the competition model for model, but it also offered cars that were more attractively styled, skillfully engineered, and available with a wide variety of options. Within a few years, the big block E-bodies would become cultural outcasts: high-horsepower engines belching hydrocarbons. Insurance surcharges finally sealed their fate. The fact that any have survived is amazing. The passage of time has assured the E-body's place in history as an icon of the muscle car era.

The demise of the Camaro and Firebird left only the Ford Mustang to carry on the pony car tradition. It is doubtful that Chrysler will ever rekindle the 'Cuda name with the elimination of the Plymouth nameplate. But wouldn't it be interesting to see the pony car market revived if Chrysler were to produce a new, rear-wheel-drive Challenger R/T with the new 5.7-liter Hemi or Viper engine?

"AAR" stood for Dan Gurney's racing team, All American Racers.

(previous) The Duster was Plymouth's economy muscle car in the early 1970s. The largest V-8 available was the 275-horsepower 340-ci engine.

In 1967, Plymouth restyled the Barracuda into a well-proportioned car. One of the styling cues carried over was the split grille.

SMALL BLOCK
A-BODY MOPARS

In 1960, Ford, Chevrolet, and Chrysler introduced compact cars. American Motors pioneered the American compact car with its Rambler in the 1950s and Studebaker jumped onboard in 1959 with its successful Lark. But these would be the smallest cars built by the Big Three in 30 years. Each took a different approach. Chevrolet used a touch of European styling with its rear-engine Corvair. Called the American Volkswagen by many, it never caught on with the buying public and within a few years was publicly crucified as a dangerous and ill-handling car. Ford became the most successful with its conservative Falcon. Ford did nothing exotic with the Falcon, which had a conventional six-cylinder engine with a rear wheel drive. It sold for a low price, could haul a lot of groceries and, unlike the Corvair, could be serviced by anyone. The instant success of the Falcon inspired sister division Mercury to introduce its own version of the Falcon, the Comet. Mercury dressed it up with a few extras to retain the somewhat higher status of a Mercury product. It also sold well. Chrysler rounded out the 1960 compact car introductions with its Valiant.

When Chrysler introduced the Valiant, it did not brand it as a Dodge or a Plymouth—it was simply a Valiant. Even though a Dodge facility built the Valiant, most were sold through Plymouth dealerships. Small-car customers liked its heavily sculpted body, long hood, and short deck. The large, circular wheel openings gave the car a sporty flair, while the trapezoidal grille opening with fine mesh grille added an air of elegance. Chic, cat's-eye taillights were an attempt to

The stylish Barracuda hood ornament was used on the 1967 and 1968 models. The 1969 Barracudas received a new peaked hood sans emblem.

draw attention away from another, Exner-inspired, spare-tire imprint stamped in the surface of the deck lid. This last item, designed to make the Valiant look like a coach for royalty, missed the target completely.

The most exciting news for 1960 was hidden under the Valiant's long hood—Chrysler's new slant-six engine. When Chrysler started work on this car in 1957, designers realized that hoodlines were getting lower and they had to innovate if they hoped to get a tall, six-cylinder engine under that hood. The imaginative engineering department calculated that rotating the engine 30 degrees to the right side would solve the hood clearance problem. The extra space on the left side of the engine played straight into the intake manifold engineers' hands and allowed them to develop an

Formula S–equipped Barracudas were treated to heavy-duty suspensions, dual exhaust systems, and wide wheels with performance tires. The racing stripe added visual spice to the solid Formula S package.

With the rear seats folded down, the 1967 Formula S Barracuda fastback offered a hangar-like amount of rear cargo space.

intake with long-tuned runners similar to the Sonoramic Command engine. This new, overhead-valve, 171-ci, six-cylinder engine produced 101 horsepower. Chrysler also used the Valiant to introduce the alternator. This lightweight engine accessory would eventually replace heavier and less efficient generators on all automotive vehicles worldwide.

But Chrysler's performance-addicted engineers could not leave the little engine alone. They applied the three "Cs" of horsepower: carburetion, compression, and cam. They designed a new intake manifold with longer runners and mounted a Carter AFB carburetor. They upped the compression ratio from 8.5:1 to 10:1 and added a long-duration camshaft. This raised the horsepower from 101 to 148. Chrysler's engineers assembled these components into a kit and sold them over the parts counters at dealerships as the "Hyper-Pak."

The beautifully restyled 1967–1969 Barracuda came about because Chrysler didn't want to miss out on the pony car phenomenon. With the increase in overall size, the proportions of the car improved dramatically.

The 1967 Barracuda Formula S option was only available on the fastback body style. A front-to-rear racing stripe in a contrasting color was a preferred option.

This experiment in small-engine technology paid big dividends when a race for compact cars was staged at Daytona on January 31, 1960. In the 10-lap qualifier, the top seven cars were Hyper-Pak equipped Valiants. In the 20-lap feature, the Hyper-Pak Valiants finished first, second, and third. Speeds attained by these hot-rod Valiants on Daytona's high banks were well over 125 miles per hour.

In 1961, the Valiant officially became a Plymouth, and Dodge created its own version called the Lancer. Mid-year, Chrysler released a 225-ci version of the slant six for both the Valiant and the Lancer, with a standard horsepower rating of 145. The addition of the Hyper-Pak pushed

the horsepower to 195. Chrysler also introduced a sporty, two-door hardtop version for both models, with bucket seats available. Sales were good, but customer complaints were high. The Dodge main plant in Hamtramck, Michigan, was rife with labor problems and the result was a series of sloppily built cars. Production of the Valiants and Lancers continued through 1962 with a redesign scheduled for 1963. The new 1963 Valiant took on more conservative lines with a flatter hood, roof, and rear deck. Plymouth's designers dropped the quad headlights but kept the inverted, trapezoidal grille opening. There were three series of Valiants: the base V-100, the deluxe V-200, and the Signet. Each series included a two-door sedan, four-door sedan, and four-door station wagon. The upscale V-200 series included a convertible. Plymouth also offered a premium Valiant series called the Signet, limited to a two-door hardtop and convertible. Bucket seats were standard in both models. Another first for Plymouth was an optional vinyl roof offered only on the Signet hardtop.

Dodge's Dart replacement looked completely different from Plymouth's Valiant. In addition to being longer, the Dart's length was accentuated by horizontal character lines. Two large headlights dominated the front with a nicely rounded grille that featured fine vertical bars. The quarter

One element of Plymouth's plan to distance the 1967–1969 Barracuda from the Valiant was to completely redesign the rear of the car with a unique concave design. The 1964–1966 Barracuda used carry-over Valliant taillights.

In addition to racing stripes, non-functional scoops appeared on the hood of the 1969 Barracuda.

panels had a demi-peak that paid homage to the fins on the 1962 Chrysler 300H. The Dart also came in three distinct series: the 170 and 270 were the base and intermediate trim models, the sporty version was called the GT. Of the 140,900 Dodge Darts sold in 1963, 34,300 were GT models—a winner with excellent overall sales. Additionally, 24 percent of all Darts sold were dressed in sporty GT trim.

In 1956, Chrysler introduced its first "A" engine, the "Hy-Fire" 277-ci V-8, in the Plymouth. The displacement in this A engine would eventually be increased to 318 ci. In 1964, Chrysler introduced a revised version of the A engine (initially called the "LA"). When introduced, this compact engine displaced 273 ci and developed 180 horsepower. Eventually, this new engine and its siblings would power millions of Mopar products.

The biggest automotive news of 1964 came out of Dearborn. Ford took the basic Falcon platform, wrapped it in sexy new sheet metal and debuted it on April 17, 1964 as the Mustang. It was an instant success. Chrysler also scheduled two debuts of its own. On January 1, the new 273-ci LA V-8 engine became available; on April 1, Plymouth introduced the new Barracuda, but it wasn't an instant success. Plymouth had pieced together the Barracuda using the Valiant as a base. They were not as good at hiding its Valiant roots as Ford was in hiding the Mustang's Falcon DNA.

Working on a budget to create an interesting car was the challenge Plymouth's designers faced

The new 1967 Barracuda got longer and wider. The increased width allowed the installation of the larger 383-ci "B" engine rated at 280 horsepower.

The 1968 Formula S Barracuda powered by the 340-ci engines were fitted with simulated hood vents that boldly proclaimed "340-S."

with the Barracuda. Making the existing Valiant look completely different, as Ford had done with the Mustang, was impossible. But making the Barracuda look striking could be done. To do so, they added the largest single piece of glass ever installed in a passenger car (2,070 square inches, to be exact) and created the dramatic fastback design. Plymouth's timing was perfect. The 1963 Corvette coupe made a statement that the public vigorously accepted, and soon, other fastback designs would follow.

Plymouth's sporty new Barracuda and its sister Valiant both could be ordered with an optional 180-horsepower, 273-ci LA engine. A four-speed manual transmission could be added. Over at the Dodge camp, the sporty 1964 Dart GT could also be ordered with the optional 273-ci engine. Both of these slick little cars, now available with V-8 engines, offered the customer plenty of potential excitement at a reasonable price. All they needed was an infusion of horsepower and a little sporty trim.

In 1965, both the Dodge Dart and Plymouth Valiant-based Barracuda were carried over with only minor exterior changes. They both sold well, but nowhere in the range of the Mustang. Dodge sold 18,000 V-8-equipped Dart GTs and Plymouth sold 64,596 Barracudas. Ford sold a total of 559,451 Mustangs. Plymouth's engineering and product planning staff worked a little magic and created the Formula S package for the Barracuda. This package offered both image and performance.

Plymouth needed to distance the Barracuda from the Valiant and the first order of business was to remove the Valiant emblem. Then Chrysler engineer Scott Harvey developed a chassis package for the Barracuda that improved its handling. Harvey participated in road races and rallies in his spare time, which gave him the experience to develop a sporty suspension. Harvey specified a set of heavy-duty torsion bars for the front, six-leaf, heavy-duty rear springs with stiffer shocks, and a front sway bar. Harvey also added quick-ratio steering, and wider rims were fitted with Goodyear Blue Streak tires. Plymouth called this option the Formula S package. For an additional $31.25, a nose to tail racing stripe could be added in Black, Medium Blue, Gold, Ruby, or White.

The toy surprise in this box of Cracker Jacks was the 235-horsepower, 273-ci V-8. To attain the additional horsepower, Chrysler upped the compression to 10.5:1 and added a solid lifter cam and Carter AFB carburetor. Chrysler didn't forget that the engine had to look as good as it performed. They added a chrome-plated air cleaner and painted the valve covers with black crinkle paint. Plymouth called this engine the Commando 273; in the Dodge Dart GT, it was called the Charger 273.

For the 1966 model year, Chrysler invested its time and money reworking its B-bodied cars and developing the new Dodge Charger. With little money, the Dart and Barracuda received only minor upgrades. Dodge returned with its GT package for the Dart and Plymouth continued to offer the Formula S package on the Barracuda with very little change from 1965.

Even though sales of the Barracuda fell in 1966, Chrysler continued to offer the model. Encouragement came by way of the dramatic sales records that the Mustang was setting. Chrysler decided to ride the coattails of the pony car phenomenon. Chrysler also decided to build the new Barracuda in three body styles (coupe, fastback, and convertible), just like the Mustang. And while Plymouth built the 1967 Barracuda on the same A-body platform as the Valiant, it didn't look anything like a Valiant.

"With the early Barracuda, they kept drawing the lipstick wider on the lady's face," says Tom Gale. "It wasn't necessarily natural. It wasn't until 1967 that it became a beautiful design—very restrained." Plymouth's designers added soft curves with a minimum of exterior trim to the body of the new

When equipped with a 383 engine, a lightweight 1969 Barracuda was one of the hottest cars on the street.

Barracuda. These body curves were enhanced by the use of curved side glass. Curved side glass was a technical innovation that car designers latched onto like a terrier on a postman's leg. There are few straight lines on a car and curved side glass worked beautifully with the rounded body designs of the late 1960s.

In addition to being more rounded, the new 1967 Barracuda was also longer and wider. In this case, increased width was the more important of these two proportions. It allowed the installation of the larger 383-ci "B" engine, rated at 280 horsepower. This positioned the Barracuda nicely against the 390-ci Mustang. To get a 383 engine in a Barracuda in 1967, the Formula S option had to be selected—only available on the fastback model. This option, as in 1966, provided the heavy-duty suspension and D-70x14 Red Line tires. Air conditioning, power steering, and power brakes were restricted from the option list when the 383-ci engine was selected, but front disc brakes were required. The lack of these accessories was based on the sheer lack of space within the engine compartment. For $97.30, the 273-ci Commando engine was available without any option restrictions in the 1967 Barracuda. This engine's personality suited the Barracuda well.

In 1967, Plymouth handed over the sporty car segment of its business to the Barracuda. The redesigned Valiant dropped back into fulfilling its role as a worker-bee transportation vehicle with only two- and four-door sedan body styles. The 273-ci V-8 could be ordered, but not much else. The Valiant would continue a supporting role until 1970, when it cracked through its shell of mediocrity and emerged as a muscle car with its own credentials.

When Plymouth redesigned the Barracuda for 1967, they added a convertible and a sleek coupe alongside the existing fastback body style. The Formula S option would be available in all three body styles in 1968.

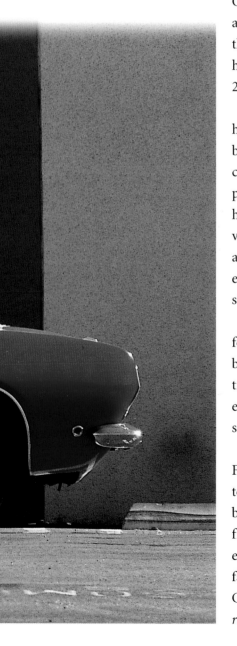

Dodge also became part of Chrysler's A-body redesign program for 1967. The Dart took on elegant new proportions thanks to Elwood Engle's firm grasp of Chrysler's styling pen. The classy Dart looked like a smaller version of the B-body Coronet. Like the other 1967 A-bodies, the Dart grew in size. Dodge took advantage of this increase in size to install the 383-ci engine. Starting in 1967, the hottest version of the Dart was no longer only a GT, but a GTS with the addition of the beefy 383. The Dart GTS option offered the same heavy-duty chassis components and Red Line tires used on the Barracuda Formula S. Dodge also made the 273 engine available for the 1967 Dart GT. Dodge equipped the GT and GTS with bucket seats, special GT or GTS emblems on the C-pillars, and a nifty set of wheel covers that simulated five-spoke mag-wheels.

In 1968, Chrysler directed the public's focus to the freshly restyled and muscular B-bodied Dodge Super Bee, Plymouth Road Runner, and dynamic new Dodge Charger. But the engineering teams assigned to the A-bodied Barracuda and Dart were able to pull a few trump cards from their sleeves to stay in the performance game. In addition to offering the 383, now rated at 300 horsepower, Chrysler also included an optional 318-ci A engine, rated at 230 horsepower, and a new 340-ci A engine rated at 275.

This new 340-ci engine looked similar to the 318 and 273 engines and had the same stroke, but featured a unique, left-side motor mount and a bore diameter of 4.04 inches. For durability, Chrysler installed a forged crankshaft in all of its 340 A engines. One of the keys to the ample horsepower produced by the new 340 was its excellent, free-flowing cylinder heads. Chrysler helped the flow by adding 2.02-inch diameter intake valves and 1.60-inch diameter exhaust valves. They topped it off by adding a standard four-barrel carburetor. In 1968, Dodge made the 340-ci engine standard with the Dart GTS. Plymouth also made the 340 engine standard on Barracudas with the Formula S option.

The lightweight and powerful 340-ci engine proved to be a perfect fit for Chrysler's A-body cars. Chrysler kept the performance package balanced by offering either a TorqueFlite Automatic or four-speed manual transmission with this engine. Road tests confirmed that this inexpensive engine could sprint with the big dogs and run the quarter mile in 15 seconds flat at speeds slightly over 90 miles per hour.

Chrysler continued to upgrade the appearance of the Barracuda Formula S and Dart GTS. Dodge added its trademark bumblebee stripes to the rear and fitted a pair of simulated vents to the top of the power bulge hood. Plymouth offered attractive stripes and added chrome hood fixtures to the Barracuda Formula S that featured callouts for the engine's displacement. Also optional on the 1968 Barracuda, coupe and fastback only, was an attractive set of red front wheelhouse liners. Chrysler equipped both models with Red Line tires that had become *de rigueur* by 1968.

In 1969, Plymouth teased all Mopar performance enthusiasts by making a limited number of 440-equipped 'Cudas. This was only a precursor to the gloves-off 'Cudas to follow. The hood scoops were non-functional.

In 1969, the name "'Cuda" officially became part of the automotive lexicon. It had been used for years to describe any Plymouth Barracuda. Now it became legitimatized on the side of the cars.

In 1969, Dodge applied to a new model the same philosophy that Plymouth had used with the Road Runner. They created a stripped-down, low-priced model with performance called the Swinger. At a low $2,800, the Swinger offered plenty of performance features such as a standard 340 engine, four-speed transmission, performance hood, Red Line tires, heavy-duty suspension, dual exhaust, and bumblebee stripes. This low-priced entry anchored Dodge's entire line of 1969 "Scat Pack" performance cars.

In 1969, the Dart GT continued as the top-of-the-line Dart model. The GT again came standard with the 340-ci engine. The GTS option was reserved for the 383-ci engine, which was rated at 330 horsepower. A handful of Dart GTS cars were built with the 375-horsepower, 440-ci engine.

Plymouth's Barracuda entered 1969 with a mild facelift of its grille and taillights. Plymouth followed the lead of the Dodge Dart and installed the mighty 375-horsepower, 440 engine in limited numbers. Plymouth also continued its popular Formula S package (with standard 340 and optional 383) and introduced two new sporty options: the 'Cuda 340 and the 'Cuda 383. Owners had been calling the Barracuda a "'Cuda" for years, but this was the first time that Plymouth had legitimized the name. The 340 'Cuda option cost a mere $309.35 over the base cost of a fastback or coupe (the 'Cuda option could not be ordered on a convertible). The 'Cudas were fitted with two small, non-functional hood scoops and a set of racing stripes. Red Line tires and heavy-duty suspension were standard on the 'Cudas, along with bench seats.

The 1969 Dodge Dart, Plymouth Valiant, and Plymouth Barracuda were in their third year of production and looking dated. Even though Chrysler had pumped up the horsepower, sales were dropping. The new fleet of Ford and General Motors performance cars looked more stylish. In 1970, Chrysler would stun the automotive world with its new E-bodies and one freshly restyled A-body.

Chrysler's success with its spectacular 1968 B-bodies provided cash to design and build the all-new E-bodies and redesign the A-bodies for 1970. Plymouth moved its 1970 Barracuda into the E-body arena and then concentrated on transforming the Valiant from ordinary transportation into a tire-smoking muscle car.

It must have been exciting to go to a Plymouth dealership in 1970. Plymouth had an exciting line of beautiful and powerful cars with the stunning 'Cuda, a nicely face-lifted Road Runner, the outlandish Superbird, and the new Valiant Duster. Plymouth offered a car for every pocketbook and lifestyle. While everyone secretly wanted a Road Runner or 'Cuda, the Valiant Duster made the most sense for many performance enthusiasts.

Plymouth's designers, on a tight budget, transformed the previous year's Valiant into an attractive car. They could have reworked the 1969 Valiant two-door, but its lines were too angular for 1970. They used creative engineering instead. Starting with a Valiant front clip and doors, designers created a new semi-fastback roofline and sleek quarter panels. This new look made all the difference; the new 1970 Duster two-door shook off the stodgy mantle of the Valiant with its dramatic, hardtop styling. It wasn't a true hardtop, but Plymouth's designers created the flip-out quarter windows that had the look of a hardtop. This creative bit of engineering saved money because there was no mechanism required to roll down the windows. They also installed one-piece, ventless door glass—a stylish addition for 1970. Plymouth again saved money by not having to create the vent window components or difficult door seals for a working vent window.

Plymouth gave their new Valiant muscle car the name "Duster 340." This was a reference to the

While this 1969 Dodge Dart looks as sedate as a grandmother's grocery-getter, it's actually a GTS model that's able to leap tall buildings with a single bound because of the 440-ci engine under its hood.

street vernacular in the 1970's for beating someone in a race: You had "dusted them off." Plymouth's marketing staff that created the "Road Runner," had obviously spent some time on Woodward Avenue listening to their potential customers. Plymouth added a "Duster 340" decal to each front fender, and on the rear, a unique Duster 340 decal that included two eyes peering out from a swirl of dust—a little like the Warner Brothers' Tasmanian Devil cartoon character. If that magic had worked on the Road Runner, it made sense to try it on the Duster.

Plymouth outfitted the Duster 340 with the 275-horsepower, 340-ci engine. This engine had remained unchanged since Chrysler introduced in two years earlier. They backed it with a floor-shifted, three-speed, manual transmission. Either a TorqueFlite automatic or a four-speed manual transmission was available as an option. Plymouth beefed up the chassis with heavy-duty torsion bars, springs, and shocks. They also added E-70x14 white letter tires on 14-inch Rallye wheels. Designers fitted the interior of the Duster 340 with a simple bench seat, but installed the leftover 1969 Barracuda instrument panel for a sporty look. Bucket seats, console, and Tuff steering wheel were optional. They also trimmed the Duster 340 with attractive side and rear taillight panel stripes. Mid-year, Plymouth offered a special "Gold Duster" trim package that featured unique gold stripes, standard bucket seats, and several other decorative features. The only engines available in the Gold Duster were the 225-ci slant six and the 318-ci V-8.

Patented Dodge bumblebee stripes decorated the rear of the 1969 Dodge Dart GTS.

Plymouth executives must have fainted when they saw sales reports for the new Duster. They recorded a total of 217,192 Dusters sold in 1970, with 24,817 being Duster 340 models. "Chrysler had always been successful in the A-bodies throughout the 1960s," says Tom Gale. "The Duster was a phenomenal success. It had a bulletproof chassis, was relatively lightweight, and had a good power train. These were 200,000 mile cars."

In 1970, Dodge kept the same Dart body and made a few minor changes. Designers sliced off a portion of the rear, which improved the Dart's overall profile. The Swinger 340 filled the division's niche as an entry-level muscle car, and the GTS remained the big-block alternative to the efficient 340 engine.

The dawn of 1971 was overcast with the gloom of insurance surcharges on big block muscle cars. Enthusiasts realized that a car that could run the quarter-mile in the 13-second range was much more expensive to insure than one that could run the quarter in 14 seconds. This shift in thinking favored Chrysler's smaller A-bodies with 340-ci engines. These lightweight cars with a responsive 340 engine were fun to drive, had plenty of muscle-car image, preserved the owner's friendly relationship with his insurance agent, and left the owner with plenty of cash in his pocket.

The success of the 1970 Plymouth Duster showed Dodge it wanted its own slick A-body for 1971.

The 1969 Dart GTS was designed around the stout 330-horsepower 383-ci engine, but approximately 30 were built with the 375-horsepower 440-ci engine.

The 1969 Dodge Dart straddled the economy and muscle car world with a wide variety of family and performance options. The bumblebee stripe could be deleted for a stealthy look on the street.

The success of the 1970 Duster spawned several new decorative packages that didn't intimidate the insurance industry. The Duster Twister was introduced in 1971 strictly as a car that looked fast.

When introduced in 1970, the
Duster was a Valiant model and so
badged. In 1971, Plymouth dropped
the Valiant name and Valiant name
plates from the Duster.

Plymouth also saw the potential of the conservative little two-door, Dodge Dart coupe. They made the exchange and increased each manufacturer's dealer stock with an inventory of saleable cars. Dodge renamed the Duster the "Demon." Plymouth renamed the Dart the "Scamp." Slant sixes and optional 318-ci V-8s were the most popular, but the durable, 340-cubic inch, 275-horsepower engine continued to be the core element of Plymouth and Dodge's 1971 A-bodied performance offerings.

Plymouth had so much success with the Duster Twister in 1970, that they offered it again in 1971. It had the stripes, scoops, white letter tires, and Rallye wheels of a muscle car, but the low insurance premium of a gas-stingy Valiant. This was because the largest engine that Plymouth offered in this model was the 318-ci V-8. The Duster 340 cut a wider swath in 1971 due to the billboard-sized "340 WEDGE" decal on the blacked-out hood and bolder side stripes. In 1971, Plymouth acknowledged the success of the Duster and dropped the Valiant nameplates from the car.

Even though Chrysler made several modifications to the 340-ci engine for exhaust emission reduction, it retained its 275-horsepower rating. Engineers added a Carter ThermoQuad four-barrel carburetor, new exhaust manifolds, and evaporative emission controls. On those cars

Even though the 1971 Duster Twister had an attractive set of hood scoops, it was more bark than bite. The largest engine available for the Twister was the 318-ci V-8.

purchased in California, they fitted a solenoid to the distributor vacuum advance line to reduce spark advance. This helped to limit the nitrous oxide (NO2) levels.

Dodge didn't waste any time getting its 1971 Demon to the market. They offered two models: a base Demon with a slant six priced at $2,343, and the Demon 340 that listed for $2,721. In keeping with the success of cartoon-like logos, Dodge created a delightful smiling devil with a three-pronged pitchfork as the letter "M" in the word Demon.

These low cost A-bodies, with plenty of performance, image, and potent, small-block engines under the hood were Chrysler's salvation as the muscle car era came to an end. In 1971, Dodge sold a total of 79,959 Demons and Plymouth sold 186,478 Dusters. At the same time, Dodge sold only 29,883 Challengers and Plymouth sold 18,690 Barracudas. The numbers told the tale as the muscle car era came to a close.

In 1972, performance engines disappeared from the option list on Chrysler's B- and E-body cars. The Hemi, Six Pack, and high-performance 440-ci engines were victims of the ever-increasing pressure to lower exhaust emissions. Even the 340-ci engine in the Demon and Duster felt the squeeze. Chrysler replaced the heads on the 340 with a set that had smaller valves and a larger combustion chamber, which dropped the compression ratio by two points to 8.5:1. This was necessary to burn the low-lead gasoline that lacked the higher octane ratings of leaded gas. The advertised horsepower dropped from 275 to 240, but part of that reduction was due to a more realistic net horsepower rating. The new emission requirements did produce one check mark in the plus column: electronic ignition. Gone were antiquated points and condensers; a solid-state module that provided a hotter, more reliable spark, replaced them.

While performance waned, the look of Chrysler's 1972 A-bodies held steady with attractive stripe and color combinations. The base Duster, Duster 340, and Gold Duster registered sales of 227,992, making it Plymouth's best selling car for 1972. The Dodge Demon did not do as well, selling only 48,580 units, but the Dart Swinger filled the gap with 119,618 units sold. Quality control problems were magnified in 1972 as the UAW continued to belly-bump the Big Three management. As always, the customer suffered with an inferior product. The bad taste left in customer's mouths because of quality issues hurt future sales.

Who knew that by the end of 1973, people who drove Volkswagen Beetles would have a smug looks of superiority on their faces? Gasoline went from being one of the most affordable commodities one could buy to one of the most rare. Prior to 1973, gasoline had made an excellent parts-washing solution for everyday auto mechanics. It also started barbecue fires and killed weeds. Now car owners had to wait in lines for hours for a rationed amount of gasoline so they could continue driving. By 1973, the days of the four-dollar-gas-tank-fill-up were only a fond memory. The thought of owning a big-block car and cruising the street looking for a race seemed pointless. Luckily, Chrysler had the Demon and Duster with a reliable, slant-six engine to sell to fuel-conscious drivers. Its other big models stuck to dealer lots like barnacles on the rusty bottom of a freighter.

In addition to the culture shock of gas rationing, Dodge flinched as the first shot of political correctness was fired across its bow. The Demon name was about to be relegated to automotive history because of complaints. Dodge's Demon had never achieved the level of success that

This 1971 Duster Twister has the optional Go Wing on the deck lid.

In 1971, Plymouth distanced the Duster from its Valiant econo-car roots by no longer using the Valiant name in conjunction with the Duster. Scoops now were part of the package.

Creating a marketable car is often as easy as keeping abreast of the latest pop culture trends. The 1974 Hang 10 Dart was one of those automobiles.

The Hang 10 Darts were equipped with white high-back bucket seats and orange shag carpeting. A sunroof was an option.

Plymouth had with its Duster— a new name (or old name) might help. Since the Dart name had been a Dodge fixture since 1960, the Demon became the Dart Sport. Dodge offered the 340 engine and a Rallye package for those brave enough to want the extra gas-burning horsepower.

Plymouth continued to see sales increase with its Duster through 1973. In addition to the popular Gold Duster and Duster 340, Plymouth added the Space Duster. This version of the beloved A-body included fold-down rear seats that gave the buyer a small car with the cargo capacity of a larger vehicle. The success of the Space Duster prompted Dodge to add a fold-down rear seat option to its Dart Sport.

By 1974, the public was beginning to tire of the look of Chrysler's A-body Duster and Dart Sport. They didn't tire, however, of the low-buck value of the cars, especially with the threat of continued gas shortages and higher prices. The once wonderful E-bodies were now facing extinction, and the A-bodies were positioned to fill Chrysler's "sporty" niche. This kept Chrysler alive and off the respirator. Dodge presented the only new A-body packaging with the mid-year release of the surf-inspired "Hang Ten" option for the Dart Sport. It featured stylized graphics depicting ocean waves and surfing themes, a fold-down rear seat (for the surf board, of course), white bucket seats, and orange shag carpeting. The Dodge marketing team that had once had its ears tuned to the street was now hanging its hat on pop culture to sell cars.

The biggest change for the 1974 A-bodied Duster and Dart Sport happened under the hood. Chrysler replaced its 340-ci LA engine with the 360-ci LA engine. This would be the last and longest lived of the LA (also known as A) engine series. Chrysler first introduced the 360 in 1971, its 255 horsepower pushing the Furies and the Monacos down the road. Engineers designed it as a medium-performance V-8 that met emissions standards. This new engine featured a slightly smaller bore than the 340 and a longer stroke. Keeping with its purpose, only a two-barrel carburetor was available. When Chrysler installed it in the 1974 A-body, they added a four-barrel carburetor and the horsepower jumped to 245 (net).

In 1975, the only sporty Chrysler cars with any credentials were the Duster and Dart. But the muscle car era had ended. Proving that fact were the miniscule sales of the Duster 360 and Dart Sport 360. Chrysler would bring the Duster and Dart back for a final curtain call in 1976. Their replacements, introduced in 1977, were the Dodge Aspen and the Plymouth Volare.

When Chrysler introduced the Valiant in 1960, no one could have realized the impact it and its successors would have on the company in the next decade. The derivatives of this A-body included the innovative Barracuda, the Dart, and the Duster. The slant-six engine, also introduced in 1960, showcased Chrysler's approach to creative problem solving. The snappy 273-ci engine, introduced in 1964, grew to 340 and became one of the most heralded small-block engines in automotive history. But Plymouth's decision to graft a new body to the Valiant and create the Duster was a true stroke of genius: On a limited budget, Plymouth created an entirely new 1970s look. The addition of the 340 engine created a classic Mopar muscle car.

The Hang 10 Dart featured a stylized surfer integrated into the body side stripes.

VIPER

(previous) *Looking like a predatory animal, the 1995 RT/10 in yellow was simply a brightly colored sledgehammer that could embarrass foreign competition costing twice as much.*

Deleted fog lamps and lace spoke wheels were visual cues in 1999 that the ACR was not like your neighbor's Viper. Intended for club racing, it's doubtful that most turned a tire on the track.

VIPER

Most hard-core automotive enthusiasts can recall the day they first saw a Viper. That kind of sighting is deeply etched into the psyche of a gear head, much like the first sighting of a 427 Cobra, a 1963 split-window Corvette, or a Hemi anything. Gear heads might not be able to remember their wedding anniversary, but they tend to catalog great automotive events and remember the specifics of location, time of day, and what they were driving at the moment they saw a significant car. With this kind of instant acknowledgment, the Dodge Viper quickly became a cultural icon.

The Viper first showed its fangs during the 1989 auto show season and the response was overwhelming. The Viper show car appeared by virtue of the hard work of a small, dedicated crew and the vision of Chrysler President Bob Lutz and other executives. It all began when Bob Lutz called Tom Gale, then vice president of Design, into his office in February, 1988. "Lutz had a fascination for Cobras and owned an Autocraft Cobra," says Tom Gale. "We needed a shot in the arm, and he'd talked about building something special a few times." Lutz wanted a Cobra-like show car for the 1989 auto show, so Gale went to work.

"Two weeks later, Lutz came down to the studio," says Gale. "We had all the packages done, and several sketches." Each of Detroit's automotive designers had a file of sketches of exotic cars they would like to see in their own garage. "We had really been working on it for some time because he

The original Viper show car that was displayed at the 1989 Detroit North American Auto Show is safely ensconced on a revolving display at the Walter P. Chrysler Museum. The similarity between this vehicle and 1992 production cars is striking.

had expressed an interest in this type of car—and that's an assignment you'd kill for." Lutz was blown away with the work of Gale's team. Chrysler would build a show car for 1989. Because of the short time frame, Gale hired a company called Autodynamics, small shop in Madison Heights, Michigan, to build a clay model beyond the view of prying corporate eyes.

Two weeks later Gale took Lutz out to Autodynamics to see the progress on the full-size clay model of the car. "Bob never did like the front of the car," recalls Gale. "We said, 'this is what we've got to do. This is going to become the face for Dodge,' and he went along with it." Within a few weeks they had finalized the look of the show car. "The concept car became the production car," exclaimed Gale. "Then we formed the group."

From the first discussions about this new Cobra-like car, Lutz determined that it would have the new Chrysler V-10 engine being designed for the Dodge trucks. Engineers would build the car around a big American engine, similar to the way in which the Cobras and Panteras had been built. "We packaged the original concept car around a V-10 from the very start," says Gale. Unfortunately, when the project began, there were no corporate V-10s available. So they took an existing V-8 and added two more cylinders. Gale recalls, "We couldn't get anything from engineering, so I said, 'Screw it, I'll build my own engine,' and we did. We put it together and it didn't run too well, but we knew we had the production stuff coming." At that point, Gale was

The 1996 Viper GTS Coupe was available in any color, as long as it was metallic blue with white stripes. Polished wheels were a carryover from the prototype GTS, and with 490 ft-lbs of twist, the rear tires never stood a chance.

A massive front-hinged clamshell hood spanned the entire width of the 1994 Viper RT/10. Finding the front of the vehicle when pulling into a garage took steady nerves.

more concerned with developing the package than with performance.

Naming any new car is difficult enough, but naming a car that might eventually become an icon seemed like a monumental task. No committees or focus groups created the Viper name. Lutz would have loved to use the Cobra name, but Ford had a lock on it. "We were looking for a snake name and we couldn't find one that we could use," says Gale. Gale asked his friend, well-known Italian designer Giorgetto Giugiaro, to translate the English word snake into Italian: "Vipera." On a plane trip back from Chrysler's Pacifica design studio, the Viper name was evaluated and ultimately chosen by Lutz, Gale, and Director of Advanced Design Neil Walling. The creation of the Viper emblem was equally simple. One of the designers had sketched up an emblem featuring a grinning snake's head—no committees or focus groups were required for a winning graphic.

At Chrysler's West Coast Pacifica Studio, work started on the secondary Viper design. They created a 9/10 scale Viper with a V-8 engine as a backup. If the money hadn't been available to put the original V-10 Viper concept into production, the smaller V-8 version would have sufficed. Interestingly, most of the surface detail from this backup vehicle appeared on the production Viper. The Viper's three-spoke, alloy wheels also originated from this car.

The Viper debuted to rave reviews at the 1989 North American Auto Show in Detroit. This bright-red Viper rotated under a marquee emblazoned with "VIPER RT/10" in red neon. Everyone was amazed that a company nearing extinction only a few years earlier had built such an exciting car. Because of Chrysler's recent history, no one could have imagined that the Viper would actually come to pass. At all the auto shows, corporate marketing managers circled around the displays to eavesdrop on conversations and reactions of show attendees. The wave of positive response from enthusiasts created a difficult business decision for Chrysler executives. Should this car be built—and could they do it?

The Viper Technical Policy Committee ensured that the vehicle, if approved, would not become a four-door economy version of the Viper. Francois Castaing, then vice-president of engineering, was brought into the Viper's inner circle and assumed the role of the project's conscience. He, like Gale and Lutz, loved cars and was passionate about the Viper. They recruited Carroll Shelby, the

251

The colorful induction system on the first-generation Viper RT/10 used inter-weaving intake runners to maximize airflow. Note the dual throttle cables.

The calm before the storm. A 1996 Viper RT/10 exhibits sinuous styling and aggressive attitude even before the engine is started. With 488-ci, it could walk the talk.

father of the Cobra, as their spiritual leader. The enthusiasm within the company started to spread. After years of building bread-and-butter transportation cars, everyone wanted in on the Viper project. The Viper Technical Policy Committee made certain that those picked for the small team possessed the right credentials, as well as the "skinned knuckles and greasy fingernails," of a person who really knew cars.

Money had always been tight at Chrysler, and getting money for this project was difficult. Chrysler Chairman Lee Iacocca had the combination to the vault, and the team needed to crack the code. They estimated it would take at least fifty million dollars to put the Viper on the road. Approaching Iacocca would be difficult, since he hadn't been in on the ground floor of this project. The group sent in Carroll Shelby. He and Iacocca had been old friends from the days of the Shelby Mustang and the original Cobra. The strategy worked. Iacocca gave Shelby the green light, and the first phase of the Viper project took off.

With seed money in place, the team still had to make sure that a secondary infusion of cash

Factory sidepipes have caught the careless, yet they have proven to be popular. Huge vents at the front of the door helped evacuate hot air from the engine compartment.

With a classic three-spoke steering wheel and a beefy Model T-56 six-speed manual transmission under the wide center tunnel, the last thing a Viper RT/10 driver wanted to see was the end of the road. Black-on-white instrumentation was a classic touch.

would be forthcoming to finish the project. This meant keeping Iacocca onboard and maintaining his interest. So, the team delivered the prototype Viper right to Iacocca's office and let him drive it. His response was, "Get this thing built!"

Tom Gale recalls, "I give Iacocca a lot of credit for enabling us to build this car. He was just a great guy and a great sponsor." Iacocca always responded positively to well-built prototypes, and the Viper was no different. His ability to spot a potential winner had always been strong, and he proved that again with the Viper. Iacocca also knew how to work a room. He demonstrated that on May 18, 1990 when he stood in front of a group of automotive journalists, tossed Bob Lutz a set of keys, and said, "Build it!"

At that time, there was only one person within the Chrysler organization who knew enough about sports cars to run this program: Roy Sjoberg. He came to Chrysler from GM where he worked with Zora Arkus-Duntov on the Corvette. Building a low-production car like the Viper required special skills to navigate the maze of corporate politics. Sjoberg knew how to get the most out of his 85-person team without straying from the objective.

Team Viper now needed a home where members could

For 1996 only, the Viper RT/10 could be ordered with one of three special paint treatments: white with blue stripes, red with yellow wheels, or black with silver stripes, seen here.

A high-drama car needs a high-drama setting—a 1997 GTS Coupe in Las Vegas. Despite the massive engine, overheating was never a problem when sitting in "The Strip" gridlock.

work without interruption or interference. The first few weeks were spent in an empty warehouse, but more permanent digs were soon located in a building vacated by Jeep design staff. Like an elite military commando unit, they moved in and set up shop—highly motivated people on a well-defined mission can accomplish much, even when operating outside the realm of their responsibility. This was Team Viper.

Team Viper's goal was to produce a powerful, spectacular looking car that could be priced less than $50,000. Bob Lutz wanted the car to be as simple and basic as the Cobra, but it couldn't be ordinary. Lutz characterized it like this: "What we need are cars that one out of three people hate, one out of three don't know what it is, and one out of three absolutely has to buy it."

The gas cap on the Viper GTS was a pure 1960s sports car touch—an aluminum flip style, ideal for quick pit stops. Under the polished piece, however, was a standard black plastic threaded cap, needed to preserve the fuel system's emission control integrity.

The introduction of the "sport bar" on the production Viper created a stir within the ranks of the team. Sjoberg wanted it, but Castaing didn't. Castaing wanted a clean, top-down profile. Sjoberg's experience with the Corvette told him high-performance cars were more likely to be involved in single-vehicle accidents where the car ends up on its roof. Although not designed as, or even called, a "roll bar," Sjoberg knew that this was a necessary component. In the end, the sport bar was installed.

The first prototype Viper, chassis number VM01, was ready to drive in December 1989. It was more of a mule than an actual prototype. Engineers constructed the body from fiberglass and dropped a 360-ci V-8 under the hood. The vehicle had the shape and proportions of the production car, but little else. The team completed the second prototype in April 1990. This car had a hand-built V-10 (cast iron) engine and bright red paint. This car served as the basis for much of the Viper's production development.

The V-10 engine was the heart of the Viper and its unique identity. But the cast iron version of the V-10 that Chrysler developed for the Dodge truck was too heavy. It was also not designed for the higher rpm ranges useful in a car like the Viper. Chrysler, with the help of Lamborghini, developed a new aluminum block and heads that saved 100 pounds. It was not designed to be an exotic Formula 1 engine, but an American-built engine designed for brute power, with a single, block-mounted cam and pushrods actuating only two valves per cylinder. The compression ratio was held to 9:1 in order to run on pump gas. The engine's mechanicals were traditional, but the intake system featured multipoint fuel injection and an aluminum, ram-tuned manifold. This 488 cubic-inch beast developed 400-horsepower at 4,600 rpm, redlined at 6,000 rpm, with 450 ft-lb of torque at 3,600 rpm. The Viper Team backed the engine with the sturdy Borg-Warner T-56 six-speed transmission and a 3.07:1 limited-slip rear end. For the exhaust, they added cast iron exhaust mani-

A cloisonné badge sat between twin white stripes on the 1997 GTS, a visual salute to Carroll Shelby, one of the "Fourfathers," who, along with Bob Lutz, Tom Gale, and Francois Castaing, brought the Viper to fruition.

folds that flowed directly into a combination catalytic converter and muffler that exited at the rear of the rocker panel.

The Viper Team chose to incorporate a tubular steel space frame design with a center spine. This type of frame works well in a low-production vehicle like the Viper. It also took less development time than a traditional frame constructed from stampings. The fully independent suspension system designed for the Viper featured Koni coil-over shocks with sway bars front and rear. A car as fast as the Viper required a substantial braking system. A set of Brembo calipers were mated to large, 13-inch diameter, ventilated rotors. The aggressive look of the Viper needed wheels and tires to match. The team decided on the original three-spoke wheel design and had them cast in two sizes: 17x10 inches for the front and 17x13 inches for the rear. Michelin developed a special set of

On a warm summer day in Le Mans, France, in 1998, this GTS-R won first in class with Justin Bell, Luca Drudi, and David Donohue sharing driving duties. High visibility wins did wonders to give the Viper racing credibility.

Dodge's familial "gunsight" grille spans the entire product line, including the Viper GTS that paced the 1991 Indy 500. The lack of exterior door handles required reaching into the vehicle and actuating the door latch.

unidirectional radial tires for the Viper: P275/40ZR17 for the front, and P335/35ZR17 for the rear.

Because of the short amount of lead time to production, the Viper Team constructed the body using resin transfer molding (RTM) composites. This saved time and weight. There was no longer a need to create dies to stamp the body components, and the material was much lighter than steel. The smooth surface of the RTM components lent themselves well to the vivid Viper Red paint that all early production cars would receive.

Although the new Viper was not scheduled to be available until January 1992, it made an early debut in May at the 1991 Indianapolis 500. Chrysler arranged to have its new Mitsubishi-built Stealth model pace the race, but buzz among patriotic race fans was not favorable. Many felt that an American car should pace America's greatest motor sports event. Team Viper came to the rescue and prepared two identical, hand-built Vipers like those that would be delivered to dealers in

January. It was a big gamble. Chrysler wanted the Viper to be seen by television viewers worldwide as the next American automotive icon, but there was a concern that these hastily constructed stand-ins might not perform. A mechanical failure would be a disaster. Fortunately, the pace cars ran flawlessly. Carroll Shelby proudly drove the Viper pace car ahead of the 33-car field with an ear-to-ear grin on his face, and a legend was born.

The 1992 Viper's press debut generated tremendous excitement. The Viper was the first authentic sports car to come out from an American manufacturer since the Corvette. It had been 29 years since Chevrolet introduced the Corvette split-window coupe—a car that was revolutionary for its time. Most of the journalists present in 1992 for the debut of the Viper were too young to remember the 1963 Corvette. They knew only of Chrysler's lean years and the K-car that saved it from extinction, which helped the Viper knock their socks off.

Dodge delivered 285 Vipers in 1992. In 1993, a few changes were incorporated, including optional air conditioning and a removable hardtop. The most noticeable change was the addition

Ready to roll, the Pace Car from the 1996 Indianapolis 500 waits for a willing driver. Carroll Shelby drove this car at the Brickyard, the second time a Viper has paced the race.

Team ORECA's 2000 Viper GTS-R took the overall win, as well at the GTO class win, at the Rolex 24 Hours race February 5–6, 2000. Drivers Karl Wendlinger, Olivier Beretta, and Dominique Dupuy defeated a Corvette C5-R by 30 seconds, a blink in endurance racing.

of a second color: of 1,043 Vipers built that year, 115 were painted Viper Black. Designers made two visible changes to the exterior: a mid-year relocation of the antenna from the quarter panel to the windshield, and the addition of a new material for the front and rear fascia. In 1994, Dodge added two more colors—Viper Emerald Green and Viper Bright Yellow—and revised the interior trim to either gray and black or tan and black leather. Production rose to 3,083 units in 1994, but dropped to 1,577 units in 1995 as Chrysler prepared for the first major change to the Viper since its inception.

In 1993, Chrysler rolled a Viper GTS coupe concept car into both the Detroit and Los Angeles auto shows. The roar of positive response could be heard as far as Chrysler's Highland Park headquarters. "This was a car that I wanted to do," says Tom Gale. "We built the show car that was inspired by the Daytona coupes and a Ferrari 250 GTO. If you took those two cars and you put them together, that was the caricature that inspired it."

All 1997 Viper GTSs used 10x17 aluminum modular front wheels wrapped in P275/40 ZR17 rubber, while the rear P335/35ZR17 tires kept the 13x17 aluminum modular wheels off the ground. Blurring tarmac came standard.

Rear fender vents first appeared on the 1996 GTS and were used on the ACR edition when it was rolled out in 1999. The curve of the vent blended into the rear spoiler.

The year before, Tom Gale had shown Pete Brock, the designer of the original Daytona coupes, drawings of the coupe concept. Brock was flattered that they wanted to build their coupe with some of the design cues he created for the Daytona coupe. "We had great backing for the coupe and the Viper group wanted to do it. It gave them a great platform to launch the racing cars," recalls Tom Gale.

Chrysler one again selected the Indianapolis 500 as the public launch pad for the new Viper GTS coupe. This time, in May 1996, it was Bob Lutz behind the wheel with the ear-to-ear grin. The month of May also coincided with the start of production of the GTS coupe. For the first time, Viper buyers would have the choice, albeit a tough choice, between either a coupe or a roadster.

The addition of the coupe wasn't the only change made to the Viper. The 1996 roadsters would also receive the benefit of the redesigns. To increase torsional rigidity, the frame received several modifications. Engineers added new, cast-aluminum control arms and knuckles for a 60-pound weight reduction. For better handling, Viper engineers added stiffer springs, recalibrated shocks, and adjusted the suspension's mounting points. With the introduction of the coupe in 1996, Chrysler had an opportunity to finally implement the ideas that had been omitted from the early roadsters in an effort to save time and money. The result was a lighter, stronger, faster Viper.

As if there was some question before you would get in the car, a factory plaque on the transmission tunnel made clear that the lack of air conditioning and stereo was as Dodge intended. Both features could be ordered for extra $$$.

Chrysler redesigned the Viper's V-10 engine for 1996. To solve some cooling problems, engineers cast a new block and heads and revised the entire cooling system. This allowed a bump in compression to 9.6:1. The new Viper engine weighed 80 pounds less and developed 450 horsepower at 5,200 rpm and 490 ft-lb of torque at 3,700 rpm.

The GTS was used as the basis for the ACR, a de-contented vehicle that Dodge hoped would see track duty. Standard with no A/C, fog lights, or audio system, it was fitted with a low-restriction K&N air filter, Koni racing shocks, Meritor springs, and a five-point harness.

The new 1996 Viper GTS coupe was a milestone for Chrysler. The addition of a second body style and the extensive improvements under the skin confirmed that this car was here to stay. With that knowledge, Chrysler could make a larger investment in the car and hope for a larger payoff.

The coupe was also an excellent platform upon which to build a race car . In 1997, Chrysler helped racers along by building a race-ready, GTS-R coupe. Most of its body panels were formed from composites and Viper engineers added a large, bi-plane, rear wing. They fitted the interior with a roll cage, racing seat, racing steering wheel, and racing harness. Viper engineers also added BBS wheels with sticky Michelin tires. Building a car intended for the racetrack meant that Viper engineers were free to ignore emission regulations, allowing them to increase the horsepower to 525 and even offer a special engine rated at an unbelievable 700-horsepower.

It didn't take a special factory model to get Vipers on the track. In 1994, there were two Viper roadsters entered in the 24 Hours of Le Mans by the French Rent-a-Car team. This first Viper made a 10th overall finish and 3rd in class. Winning this race would add to the automotive prestige that the Viper had been developing. In 1997 and 1998, a Viper won the FIA GT2 championships, and then the 1999 GT championship. Also in 1999, Vipers won the American Le Mans Series GTS

There was little doubt what country would build as outrageous a vehicle as the Viper GTS-R. Michelin Pilot SX MXX3 z-rated tires were specially constructed for the serious speeds the Viper could effortlessly attain, north of 160 mph.

Since its introduction, the Dodge Viper has been clothed in muscular, organic bodywork. Prodigious torque requires a deft touch on the accelerator when driving on wet roads.

Teams title and the Driver's and Manufacturer's Championships. In 1998, a pair of Vipers entered by the French ORECA team finished first and second in GT2. In 1999, this team finished first and second again, with two other privately-entered Vipers finishing close behind in third and sixth. In hockey terms, they got the "hat trick" by winning the 24 Hours of Daytona, Sebring, and Le Mans. The Viper moved into the rarified air of motor sports and was recognized as a true sports car.

Almost as quickly as it had started, Chrysler ended its Viper racing program. Executives realized that they didn't need to win races to get more exposure—they already sold every Viper they built. They had raced the Viper to hone their engineering skills to build a better production car. The success of the racing program improved overseas sales of the Viper. In 1998, there were 106 GTS coupes exported, 74 going to Europe. To commemorate the Viper's success in the FIA GT2 World Championship in 1997, Chrysler built 102 special GT2 coupes. Designed to look like the GTS-R

The 1997 Viper RT/10 employed a "double-bubble" removable roof to increase interior headroom.

race cars, all of these special coupes were painted white with a pair of blue racing stripes. Chrysler fitted the GT2 with a unique front fascia that included a vertical splitter and a black lower spoiler. Special side sills and a carbon-fiber rear wing were also added. Dodge fitted the Viper GT2 with a set of 18-inch, one-piece BBS wheels fitted with Michelin Pilot SX-MXX3 tires. This street-legal coupe looked exactly like the race-bred GTS-R coupe. The GT2's Viper engine also received a slight horsepower boost, thanks to a K&N air filter system.

Rear-exiting exhaust pipes made their debut in 1996, but because the exhaust system needed to be routed through the lower sills, the bulging under the doors continued.

As completed 2004 Vipers are prepped for shipment to dealers, inspectors pore over each car, looking for any imperfection. Red is still a popular Viper color.

The absence of a roll bar is a radical departure from the original 1992 Viper, but the 2004 model enjoys a modern folding top with a glass rear window. A slightly upturned rear spoiler contributes downforce, which improves high-speed stability.

Dodge trimmed the interior in blue leather and included an owner's portfolio with photos of the car being assembled—each one of these special GT2 coupes had a buyer ready and waiting to pay $84,500, even before the first two components were ever assembled. These rare cars have turned into the most collectible of all Vipers. In 1998, Dodge sold 1,216 Vipers: 379 roadsters and 837 coupes.

In 1999, Dodge added a new option to the coupe: the American Club Racer (ACR) package. Dodge created this street-legal package to be tough enough to race in certain classes, but tame enough for the street. The engine on the ACR-optioned Vipers had the same 10 horsepower upgrades as the 1998 GT2 models. To help with traction, the ACR versions were fitted with 18-inch BBS wheels and Michelin Pilot Sport tires. Koni racing shocks were added along with special springs that lowered the Viper by one inch. The front driving lights were removed and replaced with vents for the front brakes. When the ACR option was selected, the audio and air conditioning systems were dropped, but could be added for an additional $910.

Several small improvements were added to 1999 Vipers, the most noticeable being the new 18-inch wheels. Dodge added aluminum trim to the interior, along with a new shift knob and Cognac Connolly leather interior. In 1999, the Viper RT/10 roadster listed for $68,725.00 and the GTS coupe for $68,225.00. The ACR gentlemen's racer package added an additional $10,000 to the sticker. Prices had risen since its 1992 debut, but the Viper was a much better car and well worth the money. When compared to European supercars, the Viper was a bargain.

A Viper again grabbed everyone's attention at the 2000 auto shows. This time Dodge created a refined GTS/R coupe, with many cues, such as a larger rear wing and a small scoop in the center of the roof, taken directly from the GTS-R race car. This prototype took three years to develop from concept to show turntable.

Dodge continued to sell its muscular Viper RT/10, GTS coupe and ACR coupe through 2002. The final 2002 GTS coupe rolled off the Conner Avenue assembly line on July 1, 2002. It was the last of 360 special "Final Edition" GTS coupes built on the 2000 platform. These unique coupes were built for loyal Viper owners who asked for a special car to commemorate the end of this chapter in Viper's history. Each Final Edition coupe was painted Viper Red, accented with a pair of Stone White racing stripes. The interiors were trimmed with a distinctive red-stitched black leather steering

Functional louvers on the hood allow hot air to exit as a 2004 Viper SRT-10 heads out. The six-speed manual transmission is a Tremac T-56. Flush door handles and an improved cockpit do little to dilute the brutality of a hard-driven Viper.

wheel and shift knob. In addition, Dodge added a sequentially numbered dash plaque to each of these models.

When Team Viper sat down to write the third chapter of the Viper legacy, there were five goals: preserve the Viper's standing as the ultimate American sports car; build a true convertible version that had the same feel as the original roadster; refine the shape without losing the original Viper character; raise the benchmark for performance; and maintain the back-to-basics approach of the original Viper.

Team Viper's 2003 model retained the original outrageous character in a completely redesigned car. The new Viper proved that when designers are given freedom (and when management follows through by accepting that risk), something great will happen. The new Viper took its many styling cues from the GTS/R concept coupe. It featured a lower hoodline, swept-back fenders, and deep-cut side scallops reminiscent of the original Viper. These changes preserved the Viper's personality and improved aerodynamics. As an added bonus, the Viper finally got a true convertible folding top with a glass back window.

Vehicle performance could be improved upon in three ways: increase power, reduce weight, or improve handling. Dodge accomplished all three with the new Viper. First, engineers increased the horsepower to 500, with 525 ft-lb of torque. The new engine made 85 percent of its torque between 1,600-5,600 rpm. To get this power, Viper engineers increased the V-10's displacement to 505 ci by increasing the stroke from 3.88 inches to 3.96 inches. The main bearings were the same size, but the new rear-seal retainer was an aluminum casting and used a one-piece, 360-degree seal. The Viper's new connecting rods featured a "cracked-steel" design—45 grams lighter and 25 percent stronger.

To get the 10 percent gain in horsepower they were looking for, Viper engineers used a computer model of the GTS-R racing cylinder head to analyze the port flow with a computer program that allowed engineers to change port configurations without having to make an actual cylinder head. One result was to increase the intake valve diameter from 1.92 inches in diameter to 2.00 inches.

The Snake at night. Hood scoop is functional, feeding ambient air to the hungry, 505-ci (8.3-liter), 500-horsepower V-10. Xenon-gas headlamps are used for both low and high beam. On a vehicle as fast as a Viper, good lighting becomes an issue.

Though still a potent supercar, the 2004 Viper makes a much more civilized companion for a night on the town than did its fire-breathing ancestors.

Introduced in 2003, the latest generation of Viper is instantly identifiable, yet picks up where the prior generation left off. Interior ergonomics have improved, and the exhaust tips were back at the trailing edge of the doors.

This required relocation of the head's cooling passages, which led the engineers to use the program to develop an improved water jacket in the new head.

As always, the Viper was backed by a six-speed manual transmission. Even though the new Viper was longer and much wider than the 2002 model, it weighed 125 pounds less. Team Viper improved the handling by upgrading the frame, suspension, and tires. On the skid pad, the new Viper pulls 1.05 g.

According to Dan Knott, leader of Street and Racing Technology (SRT) at Chrysler, "They're chasing us and we keep raising the bar. For $80,000 and you get 500 horsepower: 525 ft-lbs of Viper torque that just reaches down and grabs you in your gut. In addition, you get the worlds best brakes. Those brakes will stop anything!" Performance targets for the new Viper were zero to 60 in less than 4 seconds and zero to 100 to zero in less than 13 seconds (as tested, the Viper SRT-10 did it in 12.17 seconds).

In the mid-1980s, who would have ever dreamed that Chrysler would build a sports car with a V-10 engine? The Viper is totally unique, designed and built by a small group of dedicated and enthusiastic automotive engineers. Each year the Viper has matured and become a better car. Today's SRT-10 Viper can be driven conservatively enough to carry your grandmother to the casino without mussing her silver-blue hair, or taken to a racetrack and repeatedly hammered through the gears at speeds more than double any posted speed limit.

This is the angle most motorists glimpsed of the 1999–2001 Viper ACR. Air conditioning and an audio system were optional; 460 horsepower was standard.

(previous) Dodge's Li'l Red Truck was only produced two years: 1978 and 1979 (pictured). They featured Bright Canyon Red paint with gold accents and highly distinctive chrome exhaust stacks.

Dodge and its SRT team set out to recalibrate everyone's expectations of what a pickup truck could be. The result is the dynamic and powerful Dodge Ram SRT-10.

TRUCKS

Automotive enthusiasts experienced some of their darkest days during the mid-1970s. The Environmental Protection Agency was working diligently to improve air quality. This meant reducing emissions by limiting everything that created horsepower. Some said that the EPA was squeezing all the fun out of driving. High-performance options that increased fuel consumption (and pollution) gave way to appearance packages that offered bright stripes and T-bar roofs. However, one class of vehicle remained immune to EPA scrutiny: the pickup truck.

In 1977, Dodge kicked off a marketing program to capture the spirit of the little boy lurking in every man. Dodge called it their "Adult Toys" program. Vehicles featured in this program included the Macho Power Wagon, the Warlock pickup, the Street Van, and the Four x Four Ramcharger. Off-road enthusiasts were drawn to the Macho Power Wagon and the Four x Four Ramcharger. Dodge designed the Street Van for the custom van buyer. Dodge positioned the Warlock pickup truck to appeal to those who used the vehicle for more than just work and wanted some additional custom touches. Dodge added wood sideboards, gold trim, and gold wheels to complement a special selection of exterior colors. A 225-ci slant six provided the standard power along with four optional V-8s.

In 1978, Dodge enhanced its Warlock concept with the introduction of something called the "Li'l Red Express Truck." Dodge based the Li'l Red on its sturdy D150 model with a 115-inch

Dodge's Li'l Red Truck was only produced two years: 1978 and 1979 (pictured). They featured Bright Canyon Red paint with gold accents and highly distinctive chrome exhaust stacks.

wheelbase. This truck offered more standard features than the Warlock, and with its Bright Canyon Red paint and gold trim, stood out from any other working pickup truck used for hauling sheets of drywall. Dodge trimmed the exterior with gold accent stripes around the wheel openings, and added oak trim panels to the side of the truck bed and tailgate. A large gold decal positioned in the center of the tailgate and on the door read: "Li'l Red Express Truck."

Buyers chose either a red or black vinyl interior with bench or bucket seats. Other standard features on the Li'l Red included an automatic transmission, power steering, Tuff steering wheel, stereo radio, and chrome rear bumper. Dodge took a page from the hot rodding book when it added "big-'n'-little" tires to this handsome truck. The chrome-plated, 15x7-inch, slotted front wheels mounted GR60x15 white-letter tires; and in the rear, 15x8-inch wheels mounted larger LR60x15 white letter tires. There was no spare.

Dodge built a unique, high-performance 360-ci engine for the 1978 Li'l Red Express Truck. Dodge engineers started with a police engine equipped with a

Each Li'l Red Truck was equipped with a 360-ci V-8 that was trimmed with chrome valve covers and air cleaner.

Dodge's Power Wagon four-wheel-drives were at the forefront of the burgeoning truck movement in the 1970s.

Production Rumble Bees are equipped with 345 horsepower 5.7-liter Hemis. The concept vehicle is fitted with a Kenne Bell 2.2 Liter Blowzilla Supercharger and Intercooler that boosts the Hemi's output to over 500 horsepower.

Thermoquad carburetor and added a performance camshaft. They trimmed it with a chrome air cleaner and chrome valve covers. A dual exhaust system led to one of the most identifiable and unique components of the Li'l Red Express Truck—vertical chrome exhaust stacks, similar to those commonly seen on semi trucks. During the 1950s and 1960s, hot rodders had installed them on custom trucks.

Dodge reissued the Li'l Red Express Truck in 1979 in a less-aggressive form. Dodge kept the bright red paint, wood paneling, gold trim, and chrome exhaust stacks, but added a milder cam and a catalytic converter, along with a gaggle of emission-reducing plumbing that filled the engine compartment. Dodge also ditched the staggered tires and wheels in favor of a set of four LR60x15 tires on 8-inch-wide chrome wheels. The 1979 Li'l Red Express Truck sold well, even though federal laws required it to be more "domesticated" than the 1978 version.

Even though it was available for only two years, Dodge's Li'l Red Express Truck proved to be ahead of the curve in terms of marketing a stylish, high-performance truck. This kind of bold marketing adventure allowed Dodge trucks to more than double their sales in that decade.

Dodge Ram

In the 1990s America fell in love with trucks of all kinds. Often disguised and renamed as "sport utility vehicles," deep down, these vehicles had the souls of pickup trucks. The 2002 Dodge Ram was one of the nicest of the new full-size pickup trucks. It offered a wide range of options and power plants. In 2003, the Ram truck offered the first Chrysler Hemi engine since 1971. It was completely new, technologically advanced, and developed 345 horsepower.

Every gear head would love to think that Tom Hoover walked into the Chrysler engineering facilities one day, saying, "Lets build another Hemi!" But, it didn't happen that way. In 1997, Rich Schaum, head of Chrysler Truck Organization at the time, called Bob Lee, director of Rear Wheel Drive Engine Engineering at that time, and said, "You need to start working on a new V-8 to replace

The concept for the hot Dodge Rumble Bee Ram pickup was designed and built by Larry Weiner's Performance West Group. The color on the prototype is SpectraFlair B-5 Blue, accented with the 1970 Super Bee "C" stripe.

the 5.9-liter V-8." Lee was overwhelmed at the time developing the new 3.7 and 4.7 engines. "There never was a meeting where we sat down and said, 'We need a Hemi,'" recalls Lee. "What we did decide was that we needed a new engine. Through a whole bunch of really detailed work, which included benchmark engines, we came down to a Hemi as the best overall fit for our objectives." These objectives were to build a replacement engine for the aging 360-ci engine for use in trucks that would meet new fuel economy and emission standards. "I don't think the marketing guys knew we were going to do a Hemi until about a year and a half before production."

"Our initial concepts were clear," says Lee. "We needed an engine that was rugged and simple—what we eventually grew to call 'elegantly simple': no active manifolds and no variable valve timing." Engineers were determined to stay away from too much high-tech gadgetry, things that not only held little appeal for the average truck customer, but that might even risk driving them away from the product. "If you're on a Montana ranch and you want to

Each Dodge Ram truck equipped with the new Hemi engine is fitted with discreet "Hemi" emblems on the front fenders.

289

The latest generation of Dodge pickups are as handsome as they are capable.

The new Hemi engine in the Dodge Ram truck has the ability to create a five-alarm fire level of smoke from the rear tires.

do something with your truck, you may not care for all that stuff. It became clear that we had a different market and a different group of drivers who put us there."

Lee's engine team looked at more than 30 different valve train arrangements, using 2, 3, and 4 valves per cylinder and multiple cams. They even brought in some 426 Hemi parts to study valve angles and how those heads flowed. "We tracked down a number of retirees who had worked on the original Hemi and interviewed those people," says Lee. Lee's team even went to the shop of a former Chrysler employee and asked him to critique what they were doing. "There was a lot of heritage tied to our early investigations."

Because this new engine was intended for a truck, engineers determined that a cast iron block would be more practical than an aluminum block. The block design they developed had some of the same characteristics as the original Hemi, including a deep skirt and a high-mounted camshaft. One of the objectives in designing the block for this new engine was to provide enough material for future growth over a 15-year life cycle. This new Hemi also had a large, seven-quart oil pan, for added durability. This was especially useful in off-road environments, where the deep pan and extra capacity helped ensure that the oil pickup is covered on steep road angles.

One advantage of the Hemi engine architecture was that it's very good at conducting airflow into the combustion chamber. The 426 Hemi had an included valve angle of 58.5 degrees. But from a packaging standpoint, that was not going to work with the new 5.7-liter Hemi. Lee's team worked several different designs to get the best compromise between packaging and airflow, and came up with a 34.5-degree included valve angle. This valve angle gave engineers some charge motion within the cylinder that wasn't ideal, so they added some shape to the inside of the combustion chambers to remedy the situation. This changed the combustion characteristics and improved the emissions greatly. However, they were still not happy with the cylinder's burn rate. To fix this, a second spark plug was added to each cylinder. "It's there for fuel economy, emissions, and combustion stability reasons," says Lee. "The hardest point for any engine is to run at idle because it's highly throttled and there's very little mass to burn. The slower the speed, the more difficult the combustion problem becomes. The dual spark plugs really help that condition." The lower the speed at which an engine runs, the better the fuel economy. Most engines typically idle between 600 and 700 rpm. The new Hemi runs at 512 rpm at idle and it is capable of running even less.

The Dodge Ram pickup is equipped with coil spring front suspension for a smooth ride and rack-and-pinion steering for precise cornering.

The Dodge Ram SRT-10's aggressive stance is enhanced by forged aluminum Viper-style 22x10-inch wheels fitted with Pirelli Scorpion Zero 305/40 YR22 tires.

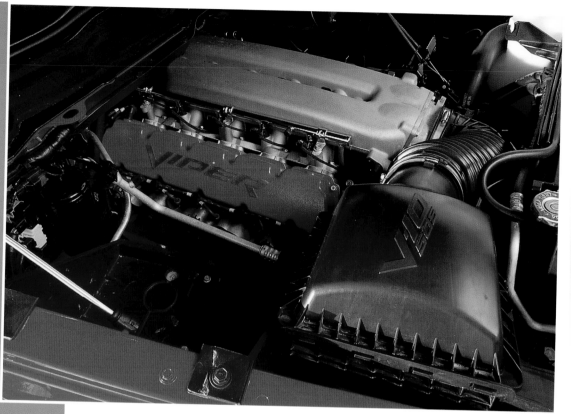

Under the hood of the Dodge Ram SRT-10 is the same 505-ci 500-horsepower engine that powers the spectacular Viper.

The Viper-powered Dodge Ram SRT-10 will do 0 to 60 in 5.4 seconds and stop the quarter-mile clocks in 13.9 seconds at a speed of 105 miles per hour.

The Dodge Ram SRT-10's exhaust terminates with two chrome-tipped pipes that peek out from a notch in the rear bumper. Color selection for an SRT-10 is simple: red, silver, or black.

In the new Ram truck, the 5.7-liter Hemi engine is rated at 345 horsepower. The Society of Automotive Engineers (SAE) establishes how automobile companies can determine the rating of an engine for advertising purposes. Presently, that standard states that the engine must be rated with all the accessories it would normally have installed in a vehicle. Previous standards allowed for different levels of engine dress. For instance, the 426 Hemi was rated with a standard that was called "lab gross." That standard allowed for a different set of conditions and with that standard, the 426 Hemi was rated at 425-horsepower. "If we were to run today's new Hemi engine on that standard, we'd get 392-horsepower," says Lee. "Whereas with the present standard, we get 345. It's a potent engine the way it is—345 is a very good number for this engine."

This new Hemi engine achieves class-leading performance in the Ram pickup truck. Though four percent smaller in displacement, the engine produces 41 percent more power than the 5.9-liter engine it replaced.

Rumble Bee

Larry Weiner's Performance West Group has been building image cars for Chrysler for several years. Weiner has an excellent sense of automotive history and zeroes in on the latest automotive trends as soon as they appear on the horizon. When Dodge released the new Hemi engine in the 2003 Ram truck, his synapses fired and he came up with the Rumble Bee.

Weiner knew that 1960s-era muscle cars were all about power and image. There were no limits on the size of the engine, the speed, the colors, or the graphics. That's the feeling he wanted to create with the new Hemi powered Rumble Bee. He built the Rumble Bee as heady salute to Dodge's contribution to the muscle car era and to the car culture of the legendary Coronet Super

The Dodge Ram SRT-10's interior is understated in shades of gray and silver. The speedometer is calibrated to 160 miles per hour. The red button to the right of the steering wheel lights up the 500-horsepower Viper engine.

The Dodge Ram SRT-10's six-speed manual transmission is connected to a sturdy Hurst shifter.

Bee. Like its famed ancestor, the lightest coupe equipped with the 426 Hemi, the Rumble Bee starts with a Ram 1500 standard cab, short bed, and is then equipped with a 345-horsepower, 5.7-liter Hemi. Weiner's Performance West Group adds a Kenne Bell 2.2 Liter Blowzilla Supercharger and Intercooler that boosts the Hemi's output to more than 500 horsepower.

The Dodge Hemi Rumble Bee rolling stock consists of BF Goodrich gForce KDW tires mated with Oasis "M1" Alloy Wheels. Just like the 1969 Super Bees, Performance West's Rumble Bee has a black, Six Pack-inspired hood. The paint on this special Dodge Hemi Rumble Bee is a unique SpectraFlair B-5 Blue, accented with a classic interpretation of the original Super Bee graphic "C" stripe.

Dodge executives liked the Performance West Group's Rumble Bee concept so well that they asked to turn it into a production vehicle. In the Spring of 2004, the first Rumble Bees were shipped to dealers. Dodge produced the 2004 Dodge Ram 1500 Rumble Bee in two colors: Black or Solar Yellow. Designers added the contrasting bumblebee stripes across the rear of the bed in either Solar Yellow or Black with the Rumble Bee logo. In addition to the 345-horsepower Hemi engine, Dodge added a body-color hood scoop, brushed aluminum fuel filler door, body-color taillight guards, and chrome exhaust tip. Available as an option were 20-inch-diameter, polished aluminum wheels

SRT-10 Ram

Like so many Chrysler programs, the Viper-powered Dodge Ram SRT-10 came out of a sketch that became a concept truck for the 2002 North American Auto Show. With favorable response, Chrysler's SRT group looked at what they had to do to create a production version. Durability was the first concern. The Ram SRT-10 engineers worked with Tremec, the supplier of the six-speed manual transmission, to make a few modifications because of the weight difference between the Viper and Ram SRT-10. The Viper V-10 engine oil pan required some modification in order to clear the front axle. Pickup trucks, like the Dodge Ram, are typically weight biased to the front. Adding massive amounts of torque to this type of vehicle can create enough wheel hop to blur vision and chip teeth. "We looked at a lot of different things," says Dan Knott, director of SRT. "We looked at a ladder bar and a couple of different ideas. We came up with a half-leaf, under-slung spring." Engineers then added a snubber on the top of the leaf spring and a power-hop dampener on top of the differential. "It works extremely well," says Knott. "As the differential starts to come up, it engages the snubber and then engages the power-hop dampener." To get the 525 ft-lb of torque to the ground, Pirelli Scorpion Zero 305/40 YR 22 tires were mounted on 10-inch-wide, 22-inch-diameter, polished aluminum wheels. "Pirelli has been out of the U.S. market for a while and they were looking for that opportunity to come back," says Knott. "What they were really looking for was a vehicle that would make a performance statement."

Wheels and tires are only half of the Ram SRT-10's stance equation. SRT engineers lowered the Ram SRT-10 one inch in the front and two inches in the rear. Bilstein shocks were added along with a rear sway bar. "We also increased the brakes," says Knott. "We have 15-inch diameter rotors in the front and 14s in the rear and we used the more aggressive Viper pads." The SRT-10's big front and rear TRW calipers are painted red.

Between the power hop dampening, finely tuned suspension, and massive tires, the Dodge Ram SRT-10 delivers some pretty impressive performance. The trip from zero to 60 miles per hour flashes by in a short 5.2 seconds. The quarter-mile can be run in 13.8 seconds with a terminal speed of 106 miles per hour. These are Hemi 'Cuda times—from a 5,100 pound truck. The top speed is listed as "150+" miles per hour.

The exterior modifications to the Ram SRT-10 are subtle. Most were done as functional aerodynamic alterations. Dodge designers added new front fascia with a black mesh grille in the back of the functional openings. The hood has a functional Viper-style scoop that is also backed with the black mesh. Over the rear of the bed is a basket-handle wing. The Ram SRT-10 is only available in Red, Black, or Silver.

Dominating the Ram SRT-10's interior is the big Hurst shifter for the six-speed manual transmission. There is no automatic transmission option. "An automatic is a sellout," exclaims Knott. "If I'm staying true to the strategy of what were trying to do, you won't see automatics on this type of vehicle."

Dodge Ram trucks are named for the ram, a symbol of durability and dependability. "Job-rated" is a term first coined 60 years ago and is still used to describe Dodge Ram trucks today. In 1978, Dodge created the performance truck market with its Li'l Red Express Truck. For 2005, there are Hemi and Viper powered pickups.

From Concept to the Street:

PROWLER, PT CRUISER, NEON SRT-4

When Chrysler decided to make a PT Cruiser convertible, they had to re-engineer the body for more rigidity. They also converted it into a two-door and added a body-colored sport bar.

From Concept to the Street:

PROWLER, PT CRUISER, NEON SRT-4

Over the past two decades, Chrysler has developed into one of the premier builders of concept cars. Ideas once swirling around in the far corners of designers' heads have been transformed into engines, wheels, and VIN numbers. A visit to a car show today is a look into Chrysler's crystal ball. The success of the Chrysler's concept cars has transformed a company on the brink of disaster into a powerhouse of car design.

Prowler

Chrysler debuted the Prowler at the 1993 North American Auto Show in Detroit. It featured a rakish, all-aluminum roadster body and front wheels covered by motorcycle fenders. Chrysler chose a 3.5-liter, V-6 engine for power with a four-speed automatic transaxle. The Prowler concept car displayed at the auto show looked dealer-ready, right down to dual air bags and a high-mount stoplight. In 1997, the Prowler again appeared at the Detroit auto show. This time it was a production version that would grace Plymouth dealers later in the year. This teaser sent potential buyers and speculators to the dealerships to place advanced orders.

To keep costs down, many of the Prowler's components were borrowed from other car lines. This keeps with the long standing hot rod tradition of using what's best to create a street machine. The 24-valve, 3.5-liter, SOHC, V-6 engine came from the LH sedan. Some were disappointed that a

All Prowlers were equipped with special composite aerodynamic quad projector beam headlights that are mounted to the sides of the grille. Five-spoke mag wheels were standard on all Prowlers.

Even though it was painted other colors, Prowler Purple is the color most highly identified with the Prowler. Halko-sytle headrests can be seen poking over the rear deck.

larger V-8 wasn't stuffed under the Prowler's narrow hood, but a V-8 required too many adaptations of the design. The little V-6 gave the Prowler acceptable performance, with zero-to-60 times of just over 7 seconds. This car was not intended to be another Viper, but rather, a gentleman's hot rod, complete with leather seats, air conditioning, and convertible top.

The biggest change in the new 1999 Prowler was an upgrade of the engine to an all-aluminum 3.5-liter V-6. Chrysler developed a 253-horsepower, high-performance version that had been used in the 1999 Chrysler 300M and LHS sedans. With this new engine, the Prowler's zero-to-60 times dropped to 6.3 seconds. Three new colors were added in 1999: Prowler Yellow, Prowler Red, and

The 3.5-liter V-6 in
Performance West's
Prowler has been given
a horsepower boost
with the addition of a
Paxton supercharger.

The Prowler's cozy twin low-back bucket seats are covered in leather. The transmission is a rear-mounted electronically-controlled four-speed automatic. Tucked into this snug interior is a CD player with seven speakers.

Prowler Black. In 2000, Prowler Purple and Prowler Yellow were discontinued and Prowler Silver was added.

The last run of Prowlers were painted Deep Candy Red Pearl. On February 15, 2002, Chrysler built its very last Prowler. They painted it a High-Voltage Blue—the only Prowler painted this special color. It featured an anodized frame, a special taupe leather interior, a unique hood badge, and a matching trailer. The entire Prowler team signed the undercarriage of the car, which was promptly donated to the National Multiple Sclerosis Society for auction. On May 18, 2002, this car fetched $175,000 at Christie's Auction House in Manhattan. This was a fitting final chapter to the amazing story of a uniquely American car.

PT Cruiser

Chrysler chairman Bob Eaton once described the PT Cruiser as a "segment buster," a vehicle that offered a high degree of utility in an economical, fresh package. The PT Cruiser's roots date back to 1997 when Chrysler introduced the Plymouth Pronto concept. Chrysler designed the Pronto to illustrate the idea of a smaller, taller mini van with extreme functionality. This type of vehicle was popular in Europe, but hadn't found an audience in the U.S. The concept made sense, and had been explored by Chrysler as early as 1994 in the wild Plymouth Expresso show vehicle.

The only way to give a small car more capacity is to raise the roof, since making it longer or wider only creates a bigger car. Taller cars provide the driver with better visibility and the perception of being less vulnerable to bigger cars on the road. Unfortunately, the American public did not like the looks of the Pronto. Chrysler did not want to shrink a current mini van, nor did they want to go in a futuristic direction. The Chrysler design team was struggling.

Designers knew that another "box with four wheels" would not sell. In the mid-1990s, retro styling themes were visible everywhere. The most notable of these was the new Volkswagen Beetle.

Its look of free-standing fenders gave the car an image from the past. Chrysler's designers began exploring these shapes. Bob Lutz loved the look of the 1930s sedans, but a strict knock-off would not work in the modern market. This new vehicle required the retro look of an old sedan combined with the modern touches of a hot rod.

Bryan Nesbitt, recently graduated from the Art Center College of Design in Pasadena, California designed what would be the PT Cruiser. The biggest challenge was trying to combine the carrying capacity of a small truck with the body design of a passenger car. His sketches included prominent fender forms, a forward slanted roof, and a wide stance—very important in a hot rod. Another difficult area to design was the front end. Cars of the thirties were rear drive with narrow hoods. This new car was going to be a front-wheel-drive vehicle with the look of a rear-wheel drive.

In addition to the contoured fenders, Nesbitt flared out the rocker panel sill to give the visual impression that there was a running board between the fenders. To keep the car from looking boxy and give it a raked look, Nesbitt slanted the roof forward. The blacked-out B- and C-pillars disappear between the blacked-out side glass.

The overall shape of the PT Cruiser is enhanced by its details. The rear, fender-mounted taillights have the shape of 1939 Ford teardrop lights, a hot rodder's favorite. The door handles are

The Prowler proved such a perfect platform for a custom hot rod that it's surprising Chrysler never offered a Performance West–style option package.

When the Prowler was designed, many elements of the hot rod world were incorporated into its imagery. The most obvious is the use of "big 'n' little tires."

large and chrome plated with a pushbutton release. The gap between the clamshell hood and front fenders is carried all the way around the vehicle with a narrow, crisp character line that completely disguises the hood opening. Cars from the 1930s had beam-style bumpers that stood out from the body and fenders, so the PT Cruiser's bumpers follow suit.

No one is disappointed when they open the door of a PT Cruiser. Its interior is as well-planned and interesting as the exterior. From the PT Cruiser's driver's seat, one has a sense of commanding the road. Because of the vehicle's height, the rear seat passengers have ample head and leg room, even though their seats are slightly higher than the front seats. Chrysler calls this "theatre seating." There's room for three in the rear, and the 65/35 split seats can be easily removed to create additional load-carrying capacity. The PT Cruiser's instrument panel design is retro-hot rod: two symmetrical, body-color panels flank the center stack of controls—reminiscent of the painted instrument panels on hot rods. On the driver's side there are three sunken circular pods that house the speedometer, tachometer, and fuel and temperature gauges. When equipped with a manual transmission, add a cue-ball-shaped knob to a thin lever, just like you would see in a hot rod.

Many think the PT Cruiser is just a re-skinned Neon, but that's far from the truth. Chrysler engineers may have raided the corporate parts bin for many of the PT Cruiser's components, but it was what the engineers *learned* from designing the Neon that they applied to the PT Cruiser. Because the PT Cruiser was heavier than the Neon, Chrysler's engineers knew that the Neon's 2.0-liter engine would not have enough power. They determined that the base engine would be the 2.4-liter, dual-overhead-cam, 16-valve four that produced 150 horsepower. Because of the tight packaging, a new intake manifold had to be designed.

Many of the components from the Neon's MacPherson strut front suspension were used in the PT Cruiser. But on the rear, MacPherson struts would have intruded into the passenger compartment, so Chrysler's designers used a twist-beam axle in the rear. A pair of trailing arms with coil springs supported the rear axle, aligned on center with a Watts linkage. This design allowed them to

maintain a low load floor, spread out the rear suspension stresses, and reduce lateral movement.

Chrysler Chairman Bob Eaton was nearly finished with his introduction of Chrysler's latest fleet of concept cars at the 1999 North American Auto Show when he rolled out the all-wheel-drive Pronto Cruiser concept car. Painted in brilliant gold, the concept car looked a lot like what we now

Performance West's Prowler hits the streets hot rod style, sans front bumpers. The removable hardtop was custom-made by Metalcrafters.

Standard 17-inch wheels and wide 50-series tires give the SRT-4 its aggressive stance.

The high-caliber bullet under the Dodge SRT-4's hood is the turbocharged 2.4-liter 16-valve four-cylinder engine that develops 230 horsepower at 5300 rpm. It accelerates the SRT-4 from 0 to 60 miles per hour in 5.8 seconds.

know as the production PT Cruiser. He followed that with a surprise introduction of a silver production model of a PT Cruiser, which would go on sale in March of 2000 with a base price of around $16,000.

It was nearly impossible for the public to dislike the new PT Cruiser. It didn't look like anything else on the road. In 2001, *Motor Trend* named the PT Cruiser its "Car of the Year." Editor C. Van Tune said, "In my 20 years as an automotive editor, I've learned that rarely does a car with so much pre-release publicity actually live up to the hype. But guess what? This one exceeds it. The Chrysler PT Cruiser not only looks great, it is great—and at a phenomenal price, to boot. It was the hands-down winner of our 2001 Car of the Year."

Then on March 27, 2002, at the New York Auto Show, Chrysler announced that there would be a 215-horsepower, turbo-charged version of the PT Cruiser for 2003. Chrysler didn't simply bolt on a turbo charger, but integrated one into a redesigned, 2.4-liter DOHC engine. Improvements in the engine's cooling and oiling systems add to its durability and reliability. Chrysler also upgraded the transmission systems backing the turbo engine. The standard transmission for the turbo engine was a five-speed Getrag 288S transaxle, with an optional four-speed automatic "AutoStick," which allows the driver the convenience of an automatic with the feel of a manual transmission. The turbo PT Cruiser (designated the GT model) is also equipped with a performance-tuned suspension, four-wheel disc brakes with ABS, and large, P205/50HR17 tires on 5-spoke aluminum wheels. Also included are special seats, a 140-mile-per-hour speedometer, silver gauge faces, and unique front and rear fascias.

The stock PT Cruiser GT accelerates from zero to 60 miles per hour in 7.5 seconds and runs quarter-mile elapsed times of 15.8 seconds. A quick visit to the Mopar parts catalog is all that's required for a better-cornering and faster PT Cruiser turbo. Stage 1, 2, and 3 suspension and turbo

Tucked behind the blacked-out mesh on the front facia is the SRT-4's intercooler.

The PT Cruiser has lines that are reminiscent of a 1930s-era sedan. Chrysler's challenger was to make the PT Cruiser with the look of the past, but with modern safety and convenience features.

The turbocharged PT Cruiser GT is equipped with a performance-tuned suspension, four-wheel disc brakes with ABS, and large P205/50HR17 tires on five-spoke aluminum wheels.

upgrades are available, along with a Hurst short-throw shifter, and several "cat-back" exhaust systems.

Chrysler toyed with variations of the PT Cruiser, including a panel truck version, woody, and two-door coupe. After the 2001 New York auto show, Chrysler announced it would start building a convertible version that would be available in 2004. To create the new PT Cruiser convertible, Chrysler re-engineered the body for more rigidity, converted the four-door to a two-door, and added a sport bar which contained a pair of dome lights. The PT Cruiser convertible still boasted 7.4 cubic feet of standard luggage space that can be expanded to 13.3 cubic feet with the rear seats removed. Additional interior room can be created with nine different seat configurations. A heated glass rear window comes with the fabric power top. With prices starting at just under $20,000, the PT Cruiser convertible is the lowest priced four-passenger convertible in America.

SRT-4

Introduced in early 1994 as a 1995 model, Chrysler launched its Neon as the next-generation compact. The Neon, like the 1960 Valiant, wasn't badged as a Plymouth or Dodge—it was simply a Neon sold by both divisions. Chrysler initially released a four-door. A two-door became available later in 1994. There were three levels of trim: Neon, Neon Highline, and Neon Sport. Chrysler offered two versions of its 2.0-liter, four-cylinder engine in the Neon: a base engine at 132 horsepower and an optional engine at 150 horsepower.

Chrysler offered several levels of a competition package called ACR (American Club Racing) for the new Neon. This package included four-wheel disc brakes, fast-ratio steering, heavy-duty suspension, a tachometer, and cast aluminum wheels with P185/60HR14 tires. The Neon ACR proved to be an excellent package and won the SCCA's Class C showroom stock title three years in a row.

In 1998, giddy with its success in SCCA, Chrysler updated the Neon and added the R/T option. Designers added "Viper stripes" on top of Flame Red, Intense Blue, or Bright White paint. The R/T performance theme included special bucket seats, a leather-wrapped steering wheel and shift knob, heavy-duty suspension, four wheel disc brakes, fast ratio steering, and polished aluminum wheels. The ACR Competition Group also remained on the Neon's option list. With the emerging explosion of the tuner market, Chrysler saw the graffiti on the wall: soon the two-door coupe and the Plymouth brand name would both be extinct. In 2002, the Neon officially became a Dodge.

At the 1998 Specialty Equipment Manufacturers Association (SEMA) show, Tom Gale noticed the developing trend of adding a performance package to compact sport cars. Gale quickly formed a group of young engineers to develop a car for the next SEMA show. Members of this team shared youth, hands-on mechanical experience, and the appreciation of this rare opportunity to create a special car. In November 1999, a souped-up Neon was on the SEMA show floor. The response

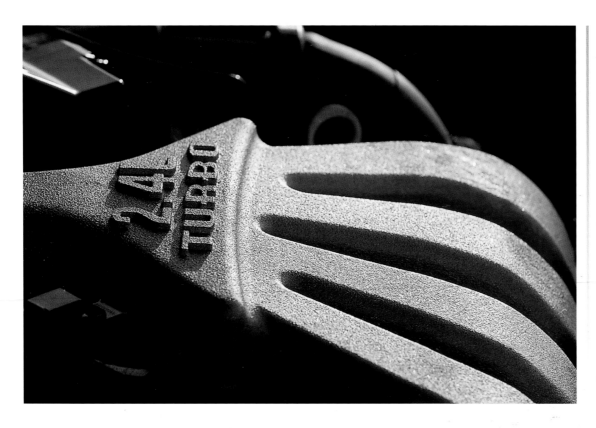

The PT Cruiser's turbocharged
2.4-liter engine is equipped with a
cast-aluminum intake manifold with
a "2.4L Turbo" logo cast-in.

The PT Cruiser's liftgate opens to a
passenger compartment that can be
easily reconfigured. The taillights are
reminiscent of a 1939 Ford teardrop.

encouraged Gale to include it in the 2000 Los Angeles Auto Show. Badged the Neon SRT, the next and most difficult step would be to make a production version.

In March 2001, John Fernandez, director of Chrysler's Performance Vehicle Operations (PVO), took responsibility for the production SRT-4. He also assembled a team of young enthusiasts to develop the production car inspired by the street-racing scene. Within 21 months, the first 2003 SRT-4 rolled off the assembly line in Belvidere, Illinois.

Fernandez's team of PVO engineers created a compact hot rod that went from zero to 60 in 5.8 seconds for less than $20,000. The turbocharged 2.4 liter four-cylinder engine produced 215 horsepower and 245 ft-lb of torque. The PVO team mated the responsive engine (with a heavy-duty, five-speed, manual NVG T850 transaxle) with a heavy-duty clutch and new, equal-length halfshafts. Four-wheel disc brakes with large-diameter rotors and heavy-duty calipers were standard, along with tuned strut and spring assemblies. Sticky, 50-series tires mount on 17-inch-diameter aluminum wheels.

PVO added a new hood, basket-handle rear spoiler, special front and rear facias, and sill-mounted ground effects to give the SRT-4 an aggressive look. Inside they added Viper-style bucket seats, a carbon-fiber-texture leather steering wheel and shift boot, along with a turbo boost gauge.

Comparisons can easily be drawn between the SRT-4 and the first Road Runner and Super Bee: cars designed to be inexpensive performance cars capable of running the quarter mile in the low-14-second range at 100 miles per hour. And with a base price of less than $20,000, the new SRT-4 easily meets that benchmark—and also reach a top speed of 148 miles per hour, stop on a dime, hold .85g on the skidpad, and sip gas on the highway at the rate of 30 miles per gallon.

For 2004, the SRT team upped the horsepower to 230. "To get the extra horsepower, we increased the fuel flow by 10 percent through the fuel injectors and did some recalibration," says current SRT Director Dan Knott. "We also took advantage of some of the boost characteristics." For more power, all that's needed is a Mopar catalog filled with engine upgrade kits for the SRT-4. The Stage 1 kit increases the horsepower to 240; the Stage 2 kit can produce as much as 280 horsepower; and the Stage 3 kit has an estimated horsepower rating of 300. In addition, Mopar offers a short-throw shifter conversion, performance spring kits that will lower the car by an inch, and powder- or ceramic-coated valve covers and intake manifolds to dress up the engine.

The SRT-4 is like a muscular arm waiting for a tattoo. "We're really focused on this idea that the SRT-4 is a palette of expression," says Knott. "That's what the tuner market is all about. That's why, although the exterior is aggressive, we haven't gone to the other end of the spectrum where they can't personalize it. So that's where the Mopar Performance Parts arena comes in. It allows the driver to take the Neon SRT-4 to the next level."

It is difficult to describe how much fun it is to drive an SRT-4. When you get behind the wheel, you experience an overwhelming desire to turn your baseball hat around backwards. The SRT-4 doesn't have brutal torque, but it provides a steady pull between 3200 and 4200 rpm. The exhaust note is more Indy car than economy car. It urges the driver to go through the gears just to hear the exhaust and watch the needle on the boost gauge dance. It doesn't take much to spin the big front wheels all the way through first gear. The SRT-4 will outrun a vintage muscle car and while doing so, the driver can play a CD, get 30 miles to the gallon, and keep cool with the air conditioner running. The SRT-4 is the performance bargain of the decade.

The PT Cruiser convertible has 7.4 cubic feet of standard luggage space that can be expanded to 13.3 cubic feet with the rear seats removed. A heated glass rear window is included with the power fabric top.

CROSSFIRE

The Crossfire's smoothly
rounded boat-tail blends well
with its taillights.

CROSSFIRE

DaimlerChrysler first exhibited the Crossfire show car at the North American International Auto Show in January 2001, and later at the Geneva Motor Show in March 2002. The overwhelmingly positive response encouraged DaimlerChrysler to assemble a group of engineers to determine if this car could be built with components already on hand in the portfolio of the merged Chrysler and Dainler Benz companies. It would be the first of many cars to be built using the best from both companies.

The original Crossfire show car began as a design exercise to develop a concept car for the 2001 auto show season. Built by Metalcrafters in California on a unique platform, it featured a supercharged Chrysler 2.7-liter V-6 engine. When first built, there was no intention to build a production version of the car. But once shown to the company's senior management and general public, it was clear that this car was something special.

The Crossfire team was formed within Chrysler's Advanced Vehicle Engineering group, and directed to build the production car to look as much like the show car as possible—in a short 24 months. Chrysler wanted to launch the production coupe in January 2003. Crossfire Project Leader Art Anderson and his small team of advanced engineers had to use existing components to build a car with the required durability and functionality at such an accelerated pace. Using proven engines and transmissions also shortened the time required to get emission certifications.

The Crossfire started out as a
concept car and within a few years
went into production. It's Chrysler's
first two-seat sports car.

What is referred to as the "boat tail" was a strong characteristic of the show car and has been carried onto the production version, where it was widened slightly to allow for a useable liftgate. The concept car had exceptionally large wheels and tires; the production version carries large, but functional, 18- and 19-inch diameter wheels. The concept car also had very short front and rear overhangs that would have made it difficult to meet impact requirements, so the production car was modified. The biggest change from the concept car was the headlight configuration. The Crossfire concept car had stacked headlights. These were removed because it looked too much like the front of a new Cadillac. Chrysler wanted the new Crossfire to have the "face of Chrysler."

To create this "face of Chrysler" on the Crossfire, Chrysler designers turned to the early letter cars and the new LX (300C) cars that were in design phase at that time. The winged Chrysler-brand logo was also a required component of any new Chrysler design. The Crossfire reflected many of the art-deco touches that were on the original concept car. "The whole idea was to have a recollection of the past interpreted in a modern theme." The speed lines on the Crossfire's hood and side of the fenders were an excellent modern rendering of design cues from the streamliners and airflow cars of the past. Looking down from above, a center spine runs the length of the Crossfire, starting at the grille and terminating at the dual exhaust tips. Designed into

Without the marriage of Mercedes and Chrysler, the Crossfire would have only been a concept car. Chrysler's ability to raid Mercedes' parts bins of some of their prime stock was a big factor in bringing the car to market so quickly.

At approximately 50 miles per hour, the Crossfire's rear spoiler automatically deploys.

Chrysler's sleek Crossfire coupe has a perfectly sculpted body that is aerodynamically stable to 150 miles per hour.

the Crossfire's boat tail is a retractable rear spoiler that automatically deploys at 50 miles per hour.

One of the most striking features of the new Crossfire was the high belt line that gives it a "chopped top" look. It's the same pleasing proportion seen in the 2005 Chrysler 300C and Dodge Magnum. From the inside, the higher belt line makes occupants feel as though they are "wearing the car," a feeling echoed in the dual-cockpit theme: Chrysler's designers intentionally gave the Crossfire's occupants a feeling of comfort to enhance the car's performance image.

Creating a sheet-metal body as striking and as elegant as the Crossfire did not come easily. Designers and stamping engineers had to create complex, deep-draw dies to stamp the shapely quarter panel. "That huge rear quarter on the coupe goes all the way from the A-pillar to the taillight, and from the wheel lip all the way into the lift gate," says Wilkins. Another difficult piece to stamp was the door outer panel with its intersecting creases. "The crossover of negative shape to positive shape in the middle of the door panel is where the Crossfire gets its name," says Wilkins.

The Crossfire's 215-horsepower, Mercedes-built, all-aluminum, SOHC, 18-valve, 3.2-liter, V-6 engine is designed to deliver maximum torque across a broad band of engine speeds. The engine's maximum torque is generated at 3000 rpm, but 90 percent of its

(above) The Crossfire's aggressive quarter panels are deep enough to cover its wide Michelin Pilot SX 255/35ZR-19 rear tires.

Staggered tire and wheel sizes give the Crossfire a decidedly nose-down aggressive rake. The wheelbase is 94.5 inches.

torque is available between 2600 to 5300 rpm. The combination of power, weight distribution, excellent suspension design, and balanced tire sizes allows the Crossfire to accelerate from 0 to 60 in 6.5 seconds.

Chrysler designed and engineered the Crossfire with wheels and tires in staggered sizes. The wider tires in the back (255/35ZR19) provide excellent traction, while the narrower (225/40ZR18) tires in the front establish directional control. The footprint developed by these low-profile Michelin Pilot Sport radial performance tires allows the Crossfire to generate nearly 1g on the skid pad. These tires are fitted on seven-spoke, satin-silver-painted aluminum wheels that give the car an aggressive forward rake.

The Crossfire's standard transmission is a six-speed manual gearbox with a sixth-gear-overdrive ratio for high-speed cruising. The optional transmission is a five-speed automatic that can be driven in full automatic or with AutoStick shiftless manual gear selection. It features a lock-up torque converter and selectable standard and winter modes.

The Crossfire features a fully independent front suspension with double wishbones mounted to the unitized body shell. It is supported by coil springs with gas-filled shock absorbers and a one-inch-diameter anti-roll bar. The Crossfire's suspension design features anti- squat and dive geometry that produces minimum toe and camber changes under hard acceleration and braking. The Crossfire's five-link rear suspension also uses coil springs, gas-filled shock absorbers, and a 3/4-inch-diameter anti-roll bar.

The Crossfire's standard power-assisted braking system features 11.8-inch diameter ventilated front discs and 10.9-inch diameter solid rear discs. In addition to anti-lock brakes (ABS), the Crossfire is also equipped with Brake Assist System (BAS). The BAS is smart enough to know when a driver is braking in an emergency and immediately applies maximum available braking effort.

Because of the Crossfire coupe's "race car" rigidity, very little was lost when the roof was removed to create the roadster.

This technically advanced system overcomes the human tendency of not braking hard enough or soon enough. The Crossfire also includes the very latest developments in Electronic Stability Program (ESP) to help maintain the driver's intended course, even in the severest of driving conditions.

The Crossfire's sophisticated twin-cockpit-style interior is as finely sculpted as the exterior. The exterior center spine shape is reflected on the center console, shifter, and instrument panel. From the driver's seat, this center spine appears to continue from the instrument panel through the windshield and out onto the hood.

The Crossfire's seats are trimmed in soft leather with Chrysler's signature winged badge embossed into both headrests. Satin silver trim is used extensively throughout the interior of the Crossfire on the doors, steering wheel, instrument cluster, and center console. Its elegant gauges are white-on-black with a black bezel and satin silver trim ring.

Crossfire Roadster

Chrysler announced the release of the Crossfire roadster not long after the paint on the first Crossfire coupes had dried. The roadster was part of the marketing pitch that initially sold the

Crossfire to upper management. Chrysler's engineers did an excellent job of engineering the folding top and rear tonneau. Without leaving the driver's seat, one can lower the Crossfire's top in only 22 seconds. With a push of the button on the console, technology takes over. The hard tonneau opens up, the soft fabric top folds in, and the hard tonneau snaps shut. With the top down, the Crossfire's sport bars appear just behind the driver and passenger seats. Chrysler's designers integrated two fairings into the top of the tonneau cover to complete the dynamic sports car appearance.

Typically, convertible automobile bodies lack structural integrity. But the Crossfire coupe body, which forms the basis of the Crossfire roadster, is an extremely strong structure. The removal of the roof only required a few modifications to maintain the rigid body structure for the roadster. "We like to refer to the coupe as being race-car stiff," says Wilkins. "We thought that when we took the top structure off of the car we'd lose a great deal of that rigidity."

In actuality, the structure remained exceptionally strong with only a few changes and additions. The Crossfire engineers reinforced the area where the A-pillar structure met the door sill and added diagonal braces under the body to add additional rigidity. What they produced is an extremely rigid body with no indication of cowl shake—the most common affliction of convertibles.

Crossfire SRT-6

Dan Knott and his SRT engineers seem to have their high-performance wrenches in everything, and it's no surprise that the Crossfire has been asked to join the exclusive SRT club. "We took an incredible car and applied street and racing technology. The result is a world-class, confident performer," says Knott.

The first upgrade on the list of improvements required to earn the coveted SRT badge takes place under the hood. Each of the 3.2-liter, V6 engines for the SRT-6 is hand-built and features a helical supercharger with a water-to-air intercooler. This engine produces 330 horsepower and 310 ft-lb of torque. The only transmission available on the SRT-6 is an upgraded five-speed automatic with AutoStick. This engine and transmission combination give the SRT-6 a zero to 60 mile per hour time in the 5-second range and an electronically limited top speed of 158 miles per hour.

With heavy-duty springs and upgraded brakes, the SRT-6's suspension and stopping ability matches its power. It uses the same Michelin performance tires as the standard Crossfire, but they are fitted on special 15-spoke, SRT-6 aluminum wheels. These wheels, along with a fixed rear spoiler, integrated chin spoiler, and rear SRT badge distinguish the SRT-6 from a standard Crossfire. For 2005, the Crossfire SRT-6 is available in only four colors: Aero Blue, Graphite Metallic, Sapphire Silver Blue Metallic, or Black.

The SRT-6 interior upgrades include a 200-mile-per-hour speedometer and race-inspired bucket seats that offer exceptional support. These seats are trimmed in Nappa Pearl Leather with Alcantara suede inserts and bolsters. Embroidered into each headrest is the SRT-6 logo.

The Crossfire's front suspension allows for a tight 32.9-foot turning circle. Power steering and stability control are standard.

The Chrysler Crossfire combines dramatic American design and personality with proven European technology. To go from a concept car that was never intended to be produced to a world-class production car in 24 months represents an historic achievement in the automotive world. Without the merger with Mercedes and its vast inventory of components, the Crossfire could not have come about as quickly as it did. Its excellent basic package made it a natural for the SRT treatment. With its supercharged engine, Chrysler's first true sports car continues to define the Mopar performance legend.

The Crossfire's rear wing helps the car's aerodynamic balance at high speeds. It also has "speed lines" similar to those on the hood.

(inset) Under this stylish cover is the Crossfire SRT-6's supercharged engine. This hand-built engine delivers 330-horsepower and 310 pound-feet of torque.

(main)
The Crossfire's inherently aggressive stance is improved with the addition of special SRT 15-spoke wheels and a unique front air dam.

The new face of Chrysler includes the stylish winged badge. The new 300C's bold egg-crate grille is reminiscent of the original C-300's grille.

CHRYSLER'S NEWEST HEMI-POWERED PERFORMANCE CARS

Performance enthusiasts have always liked the balance of a rear wheel drive car. In the 1980s and 1990s, smaller, fuel-efficient cars dictated efficient packaging and this meant front-wheel-drive cars. Ford, General Motors, and Chrysler all developed cars with transverse-mounted, four- and six-cylinder engines; these were vehicles that could seat six and carry full loads of groceries. Chrysler pulled itself out from the depths of insolvency with the introduction of its front-wheel-drive K-cars.

The front wheel-drive car seemed to be the solution to everything from heartburn to global warming. These cars were functional to a fault—the fault being that they were not much fun to drive. As much as these small engines were turbo-whizzed and fine-tuned, they were still mounted east-west in cars that wanted to go north-south.

Ever since Chrysler had created the Viper, there had been a surge of energy circulating around the company. It was as if everyone there realized that they could compete in the market with something other than automotive appliances. They found that they could experiment—and did so with the Prowler, PT Cruiser, and Crossfire—and learned that they could build the exciting cars that the market was craving.

Discussions first began in 1998 about a possible replacement for the LH-platform vehicles that were selling well at the time. "We had to do a product renewal because we knew we had to have

With its raised beltline, the profile of the Dodge Magnum RT has the look of a chopped custom car.

something in the future to replace the 300 and Concord," said Chrysler executive Joe Grace. "We had a lot of discussion about what would be the appropriate product for the future. We all decided that the long front end that you get with a front wheel drive car didn't have the right proportions." Discussions continued about the transition to a rear wheel drive car and whether it would be the appropriate thing to do. "For a lot of reasons—aesthetic and function—we decided to go down the path of rear-wheel drive," said Grace.

The streets were cluttered with cars that were indistinguishable one from another. Chrysler wanted to build a new sedan and a station wagon that would not be confused with other sedans and station wagons. They wanted a car that would stand out and be unique in both its appearance and its proportions.

Chrysler had had a pretty good run with the LH body style, but future trends were going in a different direction. It would be a bold move, but Chrysler's new car was going to be rear-wheel drive. The new platform was code-named the LX. The four-door sedan would be the new Chrysler 300, and the station wagon would be branded a Dodge.

From the beginning, the new LX was intended to be a "no excuses" program. With any product—a car, a kitchen blender, or a cell phone—there is always a compromise between the ideal product and a profitable product. "Every decision we made was biased to toward the product customers would

The size and shape of the Magnum RT's Hemi emblem is similar to those of the muscle car era.

The new Dodge Magnum RT has excellent road manners, even in snow, because of the addition of Chrysler's advanced Electronic Stability Program, all-speed traction control, and advanced ABS brakes.

want," says Grace. This new car had to offer performance, safety, and a quiet ride. These elements were baked into the program from the beginning. "At every phase of the program, we always asked about what's right for the product," says Grace. "We weren't scrambling around at the last minute trying to design stuff because it didn't work right."

Calculating which engines would be available in the new Chrysler 300 meant deciding which engines would adequately power this size car and which manufacturing plants would have the capacity to build them. "The 5.7 [Hemi] was just coming on line within a time frame that would support our program," says Grace. But to avoid adding the gas guzzler tax, this new vehicle would have to register at least 22.5 miles per gallon. "We also looked at the 4.7," says Grace, "and we decided that the power and performance that you got with the 5.7 versus the 4.7 were well worth the trip. Then we got into the MDS [Multiple Displacement System] because we knew that we would be challenged to meet the gas guzzler requirement, which is 22.5mpg. Based on the weight of the car and the modeling we had for fuel economy, we knew we *had* to have the MDS system to get over the hump."

In 1997, when Chrysler power train designers sat down to create the new 5.7-liter Hemi, they had the MDS in mind. They knew that although the average customer desired a performance vehicle, this customer would rarely use the vehicle's performance capabilities in daily driving. It is the manufacturer's job to satisfy the customer's desire for power and performance, and to somehow deal with the fuel economy in the meantime.

Multi-displacement systems had been tried years ago but not well executed. Chrysler got it right. When driving the new Hemi-powered 300C or Dodge Magnum RT, one cannot tell by exhaust note or driving feel if it's hitting on four or eight cylinders. Chrysler's synergistic system produces big fuel-economy benefits from a relatively simple system.

When going from four to eight cylinders, the volume of intake air and exhaust gas increases suddenly. There must also be torque matching or the driver will feel a bump or a lurch. To make this transition work, Chrysler's NVH teams have invested thousands of design hours to ensure that the driver senses only a seamless flow of power. "We wanted it to be absolutely transparent to the customer," says Grace. "We think we delivered. It's seamless and transparent, but that was not an easy task."

Matching a completely new powertrain to a completely new car adds a high level of complexity and risk. Chrysler's engineers took on the task, while management assumed the risk. But Chrysler's choice of transmission to back the Hemi in the LX was made easier thanks to the merger with Mercedes. Originally, engineers had selected a five-speed automatic truck transmission. This transmission has excellent torque capacity, but also a big bell housing. The size of the transmission did not package well in the car. "It has been generally received as a good transmission," says Joe Grace, "but we didn't like the package."

The interior of the Dodge Magnum RT features leather bucket seats, a leather-wrapped steering wheel, and dual zone climate controls.

The Dodge Magnum RT's aggressive stance is enhanced with the addition of P225/60 R18 H 99H tires.

And then there was the merger with Mercedes. "We looked at the five-speed WA580 that Mercedes Benz has been using for years and it packaged really well."

This would be Chrysler's first five-speed automatic transmission. Chrysler selected an aggressive first gear ratio for quick acceleration and evenly spaced the rest for smooth acceleration through the gears. This transmission is smart enough to adapt to an individual's driving style, driving situation, and road conditions. Its shift points are based on accelerator pedal control, brake use, lateral acceleration, altitude, and any load due to a grade. This transmission can also be shifted manually.

Chrysler also had to develop crush zones. Because a 5.7-liter engine can't be crushed, Chrysler's LX engineers had to manage the space around it. "We calculated out how much distance we needed to have from the front of the car to the heel of the driver and that sized the engine compartment.

We also knew what kind of dimension we wanted for the overhang. We just put all those parts together and we ended up building up the LX with a 120-inch wheelbase." This wheelbase is similar to the Jaguar and the S Class Mercedes.

Moving the wheels to the front and rear of the car helps with approach angles (approaching a sudden incline like a steep driveway), but this extension of the wheelbase creates a problem with what engineers call "break-over" angle. That's where the car rolls over a rise in the pavement, such as a speed bump, and drags its bottom side. On the new LX, this angle is an acceptable 9 or 10

The Hemi-powered 2005 Dodge Magnum RT can reach 60 miles per hour in 6.3 seconds.

The Chrysler 300C features classic American automobile proportions with a long hood and short front overhang. This is due in a large part to being a rear-wheel-drive car.

The 300C's Hemi engine features a technically advanced Multi-Displacement System (MDS) that shuts down four cylinders for increased fuel economy.

degrees, depending on the amount of load in the car. To keep from scraping, the LX engineers positioned all underbody components as high as possible.

Anyone buying a new 300C or Magnum RT expects a well-handling vehicle with a quiet ride. The LX team paid special attention to the suspension design to reduce the amount of noise transmitted to the interior. "It's important to understand how noise is transmitted through the body and up into the passenger compartment," says Grace. "We made sure that we had a suspension design that was going to be extremely good for noise isolation and still give us the handling characteristics that we wanted."

Engineers wanted a suspension that would be precise, but not one that behaved like a race car. The suspension had to be compliant enough to provide a comfortable ride, and precise enough to react properly when required. One of the unique design elements is the LX's SLA (Short-Long Arm) front suspension. The LX team also spent thousands of hours tuning the shocks. "What we tried to do with the dampening of the springs was to create a ride frequency where the car has a float—or a glide—to it on the highway," says Grace. "It's designed to handle those small undulations in the suspension, but still react dynamically."

Chrysler decided upon an 18-inch-diameter wheel for the 300C and Dodge Magnum RT. The wheel is fitted with a 225/60 R18 99H Continental tire. "The 60-series tire was a good compromise," says Grace. "There is still enough sidewall so the tire can absorb bumps in the road, but because it is not an excessively big tire, it still has some structure for handling. We know that customers will modify the car and that they'll put 20s on it; but you really get optimum ride quality with the 60-series tire."

Chrysler's LX team built excellent traction and stability-control programs into this vehicle. It is easy to design an intrusive system that engages during normal driving situations. This type of system kills the power to the vehicle as soon as it starts to slip or fishtail. But Chrysler's Electronic Stability Program (ESP) allows the driver to push the car aggressively before it engages. This system helps the driver maintain directional stability on all types of driving surfaces. The ESP system makes the LX platform an all-season car. Not long ago, many thought that the only kind of vehicle useful in the snow was a front wheel drive car. Not any longer.

One of the proudest moments for Chief Engineer Burke Brown and the team that worked on the new LX platform was when they delivered vehicle prototypes to the Chrysler's Executive Committee to test drive. Eric Ridenour (executive vice president of Chrysler Group Product Development), Dieter Zetsche (president and CEO of Chrysler Group), and Wolfgang Bernhart (chief operating officer of the Chrysler Group) all agreed that the prototypes were the best ever built.

"At each stage of the program, Burke Brown was one of the guys who was always product-biased," says Joe Grace. "He was always doing the right thing for the car. It might have cost a little more money, or might have added a little more weight, but if it made the vehicle better, we did it." Brown managed the new LX's engineering program much like Bob Rodger managed the Chrysler C300 program fifty years earlier. Brown engineered a car that met all expectations for performance, noise isolation, fuel economy, and crashworthiness.

With the packaging for the new 300C and Dodge Magnum well underway way, Chrysler's design office started work to re-establish the classic American car. Tom Gale was still running the program at that time and had just brought in Freeman Thomas as vice president of Advanced Design.

345

With the 2005 300C, Chrysler's designers were able to take advantage of the engine not being tied to the front wheels as on a front-wheel-drive car. This allowed them to push the front wheels forward for more pleasing proportions.

Driving the new 300C is made more pleasurable and safe with its Electronic Stability Program (ESP). ESP enhances driver control by the addition of brake or throttle to maintain the car's intended path.

Initially, they conducted studies on a variety of vehicles, looking for different proportions. "There was a lot of talk about *not* just doing another rear-wheel-drive vehicle," says John Opfer, senior designer, who worked in the Advanced Studio. "By that I mean there are competitive rear-wheel-drive vehicles in the American market, but we didn't feel that there had been anything done that was a real standout, or that had taken advantage of the opportunities that they could have with the rear-wheel-drive architecture. We looked at a variety of vehicles and what finally resonated was the 1955 Chrysler C300."

"In the initial design stages, Freeman would do these great little doodles of a car with a chopped hood and high belt line," recalls Opfer. "He'd have a little stick figure with a fedora on and a pipe and the kids would be waving out of the back window." Thomas' sketches conjured up imagery from the automotive ads of the 1950s. The challenge for his design team now was to recreate that kind of imagery and to recreate the classic American car. Thus began the development of the new 300C.

The most direct lineage to the new 300C can be seen in the 1998 Chrysler Chronos show car. Chrysler's designers used Virgil Exner's Ghia-built 1953 d'Elegance as inspiration for that car. The same inspiration can also be seen on the 300C. The Chronos had a high belt line with full, rounded wheel openings. In the front, the large, egg-crate grille stood out as the dominant focal point, like the grille on the 300C. The new 300C is not as low and sleek as the Chronos—its features are more upright and formal. "Design is very much a study of art and psychology," says Opfer. "It's about interpreting the things that resonate emotionally with people into aesthetics. Designing certain components of a car upright will give it a more formal and a more commanding presence." Sports cars are designed to be low and sleek, thereby giving the appearance of speed. The more formal, elegant cars have classic upright features that suggest an air of refinement. The new 300C is much like Arnold Schwarzenegger in an Armani tuxedo: muscular and fit under a finely tailored exterior.

The new 300C and Dodge Magnum have unique proportions not seen before on an American production car. The roofs are low and resemble the style of a chopped 1949 Mercury. "We joked about the 'golden mean,'" says Opfer. "The golden mean is more of an architectural term, but it's the idea of a nicely balanced proportion. It's not a 50/50 or a 60/40, but a 1/3 to 2/3 proportion that was done purposely on this car. It's a look that's very American—the chopped, lead-sled look." In doing so, designers created a car that appears uniquely American and fresh.

The interior of the new 300C and Dodge Magnum is as contemporary and refined as the exterior. In the 1950s and early 1960s, automotive interior themes created images of stylized jet aircraft cockpits. Now those themes seem more a matter of kitsch and less a matter of style. "We needed to bring the general idea of formality and elegance to the interior, and do it in a modern way," says Opfer. "The cars that I looked at most were the Ghia cars that were done under Virgil Exner. They all had a more European perspective."

Interior designers call the areas where there is physical contact "touch points." The touch points on the 300C—from the leather and tortoiseshell steering wheel to the chrome door release levers—are all intuitive and comfortable. The steering wheel is larger in diameter than most, but the driver doesn't have the feeling that he's driving a bus. The door releases are well integrated into the door panels as an extension of the single, horizontal, bright trim. The handles have a gentle

347

At the center of Chrysler's new winged badge is a vintage Chrysler crest.

The instrumentation on the Chrysler 300C is large easy-to-read analog gauges. The speedometer pegs at 160 miles per hour and the 7000-rpm tachometer redlines at 5800.

curve and deep recess to easily accommodate a gloved hand. The controls and instruments are straightforward, with no superfluous technical wizardry: To turn up the fan speed, twist the knob right. To lower the temperature, twist the knob left. While the car is filled with many digital devices, the interface is analog and simple enough to use without reading the owner's manual. Even the ignition key switch is located on the instrument panel.

Chrysler's LX body engineers were able to build an attractive and different station wagon for the Dodge Magnum. It delivers the benefits of a sport utility vehicle, with the comfort and storage space of a passenger car, and the performance of a muscle car. The LX designers veered off the straight and narrow path to offer a new twist on an old design.

The new Hemi-powered 300C and Dodge Magnum RT are wonderful cars to look at—and to drive. Each reach 60 miles per hour in less than 6 seconds and run the quarter mile in 14.1 seconds at 101 miles per hour—the elapsed times and speeds of a vintage Road Runner. The 300C will reach its chip-limited 126 miles per hour in a heartbeat and cruise there without whimpering. It is quiet around town, but when the pedal hits the floor, the 5.7-liter Hemi still sounds like a Hemi. The rumor mill has an SRT-8 version on the horizon. The folks at Chrysler haven't confirmed or denied that, but when chief engineer Burke Brown was asked if the new SRT-8 would have more than 400 horsepower, he just smiled.

For the past 50 years, the Chrysler Corporation has been placing stakes in the ground to define its performance territory. Designers began with the C300 in 1955 and have advanced the family sedan to new heights with the new Hemi-powered 300C and Dodge Magnum RT. The landscape of Chrysler's territory is dotted with the likes of the Road Runner, Charger R/T, Super Bee, Viper SRT-10, SRT-4, and Ram SRT-10. And Chrysler has promised to deliver even more exciting cars during the next 50 years.

(**above**) The world's luxury and performance sedans retained rear-wheel drive because of its superior performance and handling characteristics. This is one of the main reasons why Chrysler, when designing the all-new 300C, made it rear-wheel drive.

One of the design elements that makes up the "new face of Chrysler" are the keyhole-shaped headlights.

INDEX